About Islam: As You Would Read in the Newspaper

"The minimum time for a pregnancy is six months. It's simple arithmetic."

Can a non-Muslim donate blood to be used in a blood transfusion for a Muslim?

by
Ross A. Moon

Northwest Publishing Inc.
5442 South 900 East
Salt Lake City, UT 84117
801-266-0253

Copyright © 1992 NPI

Northwest Publishing Inc.
5442 South 900 East
Salt Lake City, Utah 84117
801-266-0253

International Copyright Secured

Edited and Cover Design
by
Jim VanTreese

ISBN #1-880416-19-0

Printed In the United States of America

TABLE OF CONTENTS

INTRODUCTION

Interest in the Middle East peaked during the Gulf War. Operations Desert Storm and Desert Shield did more to concentrate the world's attention on the region that had any other event since World War II. Interest also peaked in the differences in religions, not only between the countries in the region but also with the majority of the rest of the world. There were more Americans in the Middle East at that time than there had been in the area in anyone's memory. It was only natural to make comparisons between the culture of the host country and that of the home's of the Americans.

This book consists of newspaper articles and clips taken from Islamic newspapers in the Gulf Region. It attempts to demonstrate, and provide for comparison purposes, the difference in beliefs and religious practices between the Islamic countries and the western world. It attempts to give the reader a perspective of the Islamic faith that he or she would not get from reading newspapers printed in a western country.

The comments in this book are, for the most part, direct quotes from the newspaper articles. You will see grammatical, spelling and punctuation errors as they occurred in print. The articles were collected over a period of five years.

If, after reading this, you feel that Islam is good for you, then you will be good for Islam.

UNITY

The adoption of the religion of Islam is very simple. Nothing is required except:

Firstly: That he believes in Allah as the only God and in Muhammad as His messenger.

Secondly: A Muslim must attend regularly to one's prayers. A Muslim prays five times every day of his life.

Thirdly: Muslims fast from dawn to dusk throughout the lunar month of Ramadan.

Fourthly: Muslims who earn more than the equivalent of 634 grams of silver are required to give away every year a portion of their wealth, not less than 2.5%, to the poor.

Fifthly: Pilgrimage must be performed at least once by those who have the physical and financial ability to do it.

The World Muslim League underscored the important role of education and said Islam has urged the Muslims to acquire knowledge and sciences. The enemies of the Muslims are aware of the fact that knowledge and science are the main source for the strength of the Muslims.

An Islamic state carries a political responsibility for the establishment of Islam. In reality, this role may reach as far as the individuals' private practice of worship such as prayer and fasting. Besides, an Islamic state is obliged to protect those Muslim minorities outside the Muslim state and preserve their Islamic identity.

Freedom of speech and participation in government does not come cheap. It requires the exertion of absolute responsibility and more importantly in an Islamic country firm adherence to Islam as an ideology; not simply lip service to it as a religion. Secularism is the very antithesis of Islam on both the theological and political arenas. The Quran and the example of the Prophet (pbuh) makes ample provision for every citizen to have his voice heard by the ruler. Needless to say all reasonable Muslims will warmly support this Islamic stand. That the Muslim system of government is superior to man-made ones goes without saying.

Whatever advancement has been made by human civilization with regard to man's role and position in this life you will find it well established in Islam long before it was even contemplated by reformers anywhere outside the Muslim world.

Islam recognizes that faith can come only through conviction. No compulsion is admissible in matters of faith. Everyone has the right to choose the faith he or she wants to follow.

Backbiting is certainly one of the actions Islam forbids.

Muslims can offer a great deal. For example, human rights in Islam is supreme. The rights of worship, the right of speech, the right of coexistence. Islam offers the best way Muslims and non-Muslims can relate, cooperate, protect each other, support each other.

Muslims today represent the Third World. They are suffering because the lack of proper economic and social systems. They have to realize that unless they see progress through Islam there will be nothing. It is not a theoretical call, it is a practical one. It has been proven that Muslims have progressed whenever they have followed Islam.

Muslims have to be very realistic and they have to be considerate to other religions and other communities. Only then will others cooperate.

You said that the Iraqi invasion affected Muslim unity. How long do you think it will take to get Muslims back together again? By the grace of Allah the crisis, at least the major part of it, ended quickly. Muslims will very soon be back to work together, to promote unity and Islamic solidarity.

In the past, Allah unleashed His punishment on a number of nations who refused to accept the message conveyed to them by His messengers. He may allow a particular community time to mend its ways. It is Allah alone who decides to punish a particular nation or not.

Islam insists that slaves must be treated as equals. They are required to believe in Allah and His messenger.

The number of Muslims in the US now stands at over four million. The number of Muslims in the US will cross the six million mark by the end of this decade. About 32 people embraced Islam during the past five months. There are over 600 mosques in the US. April 12, 1991.

We do believe that the Christians have been tampered with and do not represent the teachings of Jesus (pbuh).

You have rulings discouraging Muslims traveling into the land of war which was defined as the land where the majority of the population were non-Muslims. To suggest today that any country where the majority of people are non-Muslims is a land of war is to do Islam a great disservice.

The term "Shia" means followers or supporters. The term "Suni" means a follower of a method. The question of the role of the *imam* is the basic issue of difference between Shias and Sunnis.

If we take the term "*Jihad*" in its broadest sense, as we certainly should, then it applies to women in the same way it applies to men. *Jihad* means exerting one's efforts in making Islam known to people and calling on them to adopt it. As such, war is just one form which it may take.

What happens to us in our lives is either something we bring about or something which Allah has assigned to us. The first type is our own work, the second will happen to us no matter what name we have.

Islam is a good remedy for personality disorder.

There are now 1,200 mosques in the Holy city of Madina including 64 historical mosques.

The hostility between Jews and Muslims over the years is due to their envy of the Arabs that Allah has chosen His last messenger from among them. He did not choose an Israelite to convey His last message. They have realized that Allah has taken away from them the time of prophethood because of their earlier misdeeds. They could not forget that grudge.

Sermons have proven to be the most effective means for spreading the Islamic dawa in America. News stories articles and advertisements containing information on Islam are published in many daily papers and weekly magazines throughout USA.

Allah accepts only such action as are undertaken for the sole purpose of earning His pleasure.

Unity is now probably one of the most appealing

symbols for Muslims in a fast-changing world.

There is no person or institution which is empowered to give exemptions from Islamic rulings or to modify those rulings according to individual cases or situations.

The *matawa* - known formally as the Committee for the Promotion of Virtue and Prevention of Vice - are enforcers of an austere, often anti-Western fundamentalism.

"Fanatics are driving a wedge through the society, between the 20th century and the seventh, using religion as an excuse. Their tactics are like Khomeine's."

"The fundamentalists hate America, they hate infidels, they hate everything America stands for."

Adhering to a puritanical Muslim sect called *Wahabism*, the sexes are segregated so severely that even the zoo has men's days and women's days, making family trips impossible. Theaters and cinemas are banned so are women's gyms and hairdressers. Adulterers are stoned to death.

The only acceptable music is a drumbeat - only at weddings, and even then only for female guests.

It is common knowledge that what brings people into

the fold of Islam is the declaration that they believe in the oneness of Allah and that Mohammed was his last messenger. This declaration implies in its second part that we accept that the only source of information regarding what is acceptable to Allah and what is unacceptable is Prophet Mohammed (pbuh). Anything which does not have the backing of the Qur'an or the *Hadith* (statement by the Prophet) is not acceptable from the Islamic point of view. I can tell you without any hesitation that there is nothing in the Qur'an or the *Hadith* to approve the wearing of a charm which contains verses of the Qur'an. It's prohibition is absolutely clear because it implies that a particular object is of benefit in obtaining something good or repelling something bad. A person who wears a charm is guilty of polytheism.

You find people writing at the top of their letters the figure 786 as a substitute for the standard phrase which begins any action and which is translated as, "In the name of Allah, the Merciful, the Beneficent." This is absurd.

There is no truth whatsoever that the Prophet suffered from a magic spell at any time in his life. Only unbelievers state that and their claims cannot be proven. That is not acceptable from a Muslim.

Enemies of the Islamic Nation have exploited the recent crises and divisions to multiply the suffering of the Islamic Nation, hatched their suspicious plots for weakening the nation, sowed seeds as discord and dismantled

its solidarity. The enemies of Islam are quite confident that
our unity is a strength that generates fear in them. They
believe that the Muslims solidarity would foil and undermine
their conspiracies and defeat them, so they usually attempt to
trigger seditions, revive old spites and intrigues until they
could pave a clear path for execution of their painful strikes
and spread killings, plundering and corruption on the earth.

The enemies of the Islamic Nation have resorted to another method of wars to destroy the new generation through
export of poisons - smuggling of drugs into the Islamic and
Arab states as an effective means to pull down and weaken
human and ideological capabilities of the Muslim youth, the
most precious wealth of the Islamic Nation.

That culture and Islamic adherence is closely interrelated
is an undeniable fact. The lifestyles portrayed in TV films
gradually nibbles at our Islamic value system, making total
assimilation into the other culture just a matter of time. Culture
loss is more than giving up some routine habits, it causes the
loss of *adah* and resultantly a loss of coherence to the body of
Islam the *ummah* As the nation of Islam we will never retain
our cultural independence without vision and a loving adherence to Allah's book and the Prophet's example.

The best way is the way of Mohammed. The worst thing
are matters newly invented in religion. Every invented matter
is an innovation. Every innovation leads astray. To

obey the Prophet is to do as he said in this particular example to avoid innovations *(bida')* and follow his way. This essentially is the proverbial "bottom line".

Needless to say, the social order that Islam establishes takes humanity by the hand to elevate it to heights which cannot be attained through any other means. When Islam was allowed to have its full play in the life of Arabia, the Arab rose to heights which could not have been imagined by them at the time and cannot even be imagined today by even the most advanced of democratic systems.

In Italy the ranks of Christians who have converted to Islam are swelling daily The figures are still relatively low, an estimated 2,000 so far; compared with the nation's 56 million Roman Catholics and 700,000 Muslims from overseas. But the growth is a steady one. 19 May, 1991.

As well as announcements of births, marriages and conversions, his Muslim newspaper carries advice on how Italian converts should behave. For example he advises that a woman who intends to drive her car beyond the boundaries of her own neighborhood should make sure she is accompanied by a relative.

"But in the past six years I've noticed a dramatic improvement in myself. If you pray five times a day it also forces you to break off from the daily treadmill. It makes you stop and reflect and prevent you from becoming an automation who lives his life mechanically."

"The rhythm of my lifestyle is different from that of the society to which I once belonged. I pray five times a day, and in between those prayers I find I'm not greedy or envious, I don't get angry or violent, I'm not competitive and I don't prevaricate."

Most of those at the helm of decision-making in the Muslim World, with the exception of very few Muslim countries, have been fascinated by the Western civilization and its materialistic achievements.

As for Muslim minorities who live in a multi-ethnic, multi-religious, multi-cultural society, we are all aware that they are being exposed to policies of assimilation into the major predominant culture. Their brethren in the "adobe of Islam" should not forsake them amid currents of alien thoughts.

Muslim children who receive secular education in private or governmental schools should be encouraged to attend a "Friday School", attached to an Islamic centre or a large mosque, in order to enrich their awareness of the revealed knowledge and the Islamic moral values.

Islam takes a very serious view of lying. I should point out that there are three excuses when telling a lie is permissible.

The first is that when the purpose of the lie is to confuse

or to pass wrong information to the enemy in order to increase the chances of the Muslim army winning in battle.

The second case is when a person is trying to achieve reconciliation between two Muslims in dispute.

The third case is that of well intentioned lies between husband and wife.

Let me give you the example of a wife who makes much fuss about the help her husband gives to his poor relatives. If he comes home one day having given his mother or a poor relative some money, and his wife questions him about that, he is permitted to tell her that he has given them a much smaller figure or that he has not given them anything in order to keep her quiet.

The general rule is that a game which relies on chance is forbidden, because the likelihood of quarrels erupting as a result of such a game is strong. When betting is involved, a game is forbidden, even though it may be permissible on its own.

Circumcision is recommended for Muslim boys. If a Muslim child has not been circumcised then he is recommended to accomplish that. If he does not, then he has only failed to do a recommended practice. There is no sin involved.

On Education:

The child should be trained to get accustomed to harsh life in order to predispose him of any probable hard time in the future. He should not be left to sleep during the day time, which would lead to laziness.

The Muslim World League, based in Makkah, publishes *World Muslim News*, their official organ. The *News* editor said, in referring to the Kashmir problem, the Indian government "cannot forever endure the shock and burden of their indescribable misdeeds and savagery in the Muslim value."

The paper noted that there are supplementary factors such as India's increasing dependence on the Arab petroleum as well as on the Mid-east market and the presence of 150 million Muslims "within the confines of that unmanageable caldron, overflowing with poverty, disease, illiteracy and corruption, called the biggest democracy in the world, which have changed the scenario for the worse."

The editorial said Muslim countries are deeply involved in their own intricate problems and do not seem to be in a position to sustain or support the *jihad* in Kashmir on a scale matching the allied powers enormous and unlimited assistance to Kuwait during her recent conflict with Iraq.

"The least the Kashmir brethren expect for their Muslim brethren in the present circumstances is that besides denouncing the New Delhi savagery and Machiavellian conduct in their homeland, they would immediately snap all economic relations with India and desist from entering into any business deals with her government till the question of Kashmir self determination is finally settled," the paper said.

"You can be a good Muslim and at the same time live the American way." Young Muslims may be tempted by the freedoms of American culture. But parents can use Islamic instruction to help their children avoid such forbidden activities as drinking alcohol, dancing and dating. "I think Americas a great country, it just needs to have some more limits on the people over here." As the Muslim population in America has increased people have become more tolerant.

(Cattle, "Al-Anaam". 6: 51-54) These verses draw for humanity the rising curve, marking each stage in order to show the low level of ignorance at which the Arabs were before Islam took them by the hand to reach the high summit. When they had attained it, they took the rest of mankind with them. But humanity retreats from the summit and tumbles back to the lower depth. We see in New York, Washington, Chicago, Johannesburg and other centers of "civilizations" a latter day prevalence of the same stinking bigotry based on ties of race, nationhood and class.

"We are witnessing today a delicate plan which aims at destroying the Islamic personality. The Judaisation of the religious monuments and the Islamic antiquities in occupied Jerusalem and Arab Palestine, and other places such as Afghanistan, is only one aspect of the destructive plan. Here comes the role of the leading intellectuals of the Islamic world and the members of the Higher World Council of mosques. We call upon them all to play their role in the shaping of the Muslim wherever he may be in this troubled and aimless world, so that the Muslim becomes the exemplar of man whom God honored and made vicegerent on earth."

The Ka'bah is the only spot in the world which was dedicated to the worship of God, the Almighty, the One and Indivisible, as long as five thousand years ago.

Kareem Abdul Jabbar said that his children do not have much of an opportunity to learn about the 'Deen' because the American school system does not provide for religious education "and my ex-wife did not have the opportunity to take them to the Islamic center in Los Angles on a regular basis, so their education has suffered."

One particular aspect of Islam that impresses Abdul Jabbar most was the fact that "it has not been tainted by human error. I became very much aware of the fact that the bible has been tampered with by the generations that followed Jesus Christ. I found that Islam has remained true and pure."

Abdul Jabbar said that it is difficult being a Muslim in

America. "The environment is very different. The morality is very different from the one practiced in Muslim countries."

A leading American Muslim scholar described Islam as the vanguard against Western cultural hegemony and said it has the potential to save the human race from total congest. He pinpointed English, French and Spanish languages as the symbols of Western culture. The leading ideologies like liberalism, capitalism, socialism, Marxism and excesses of fascism are all derived from the West.

The professor said that the world economic system is heavily Western. "So the majority factor in this case is not in terms of individuals, it is the omnipresences of a civilization that is not in itself Islamic, but which is nevertheless affecting wide sectors of the Ummah, and many of us, myself included, are substantially products of the Western culture as well as being Muslims."

The scholar said there were two forces that were resisting total conquest; Marxism, a child of Western thought, and Islam. With the fall of Marxism in its strongholds, Islam has become "the main rebel in the North-South relations."

Apostasy from Islam is a grievous crime punished by death. "As for the one who goes out of Islam to something else and divulges it, one calls him to taubah. If he does not turn in taubah he is killed. One who commits apostasy from Islam rejects truth after he had known it, thus, he does not deserve life and loses the rasion-deter of his existence.

Violations leading to apostasy are many:

1) Idolatry - that is to worship others beside Allah.

2) The Muslim must charge idolaters, atheist and magians with unbelief. A Muslim commits the grievous sin of unbelief if he does not accuse such men with unbelief.

3) Sorcery is a form of unbelief especially when it includes grave idolatrous deviations.

4) Whoever believes that there is a law better than the law of Islam or that there is a system better than that revealed to Muhammad (phub), is an unbeliever.

5) Whoever dislikes Prophet Muhammad (pbuh) or abominates any rules of Islamic law is an unbeliever.

6) Whoever ridicules any of the precepts of Islam knowingly is an unbeliever.

7) Whoever longs for the defeat of Islam and abhors its victories is an unbeliever.

8) Whoever takes unbelievers as friends and give the support knowingly with abrogation to Islamic rule is an unbeliever.

9) To believe that there are certain men authorized to violate Islamic law and perform what is contrary to it is unbelief.

10) Whoever shuns Islamic faith or law after being reminded of it is an unbeliever.

11) To deny or reject any of the fundamentals of Islam is unbelief.

The greatest difficulty that confronts the Islamic movement of today is represented by the fact that we see in the lands that used to belong to Islam where the Islamic faith was supreme, people of Islamic descent, but both the land and its people have abandoned Islam in reality. Although they continue to claim to be Muslims. They disown the basic Islamic principles in faith and reality although they may think that they still believe in Islam as a faith.

The critics of Islam often perpetuate the lie that Islam is not tolerant of other faiths and that the non-Muslim must be converted; even by force. The principals of Islams understanding of religious tolerance are based on the following:

1) The Quran brings home to us the point that revealed religions have sprung up from the same fountainhead.

2) The position of all the Prophets as Messengers of God is equal.

3) The Quran clearly and unambiguously states that there is no compulsion in religion.

4) The places of worship of the other religions are to be respected and defended.

5) It is not permissible to kill or persecute a person on the grounds of difference in creed.

6) The discriminating factor between people is to be judged according to taqwa - fear of God - and beneficence to mankind.

7) A Muslim is expected to be kind and treat his relatives well irrespective of difference of religion.

8) Debates and religious discussions are permissible if conducted with dignity, serenity and respect.

The first person to begin the tradition of washing the Ka'bah was Prophet Muhammad (pbuh). This was the day

of conquest of Makkah. The Prophet ordered the washing of
the Kabah with Zam-zam water. He washed away and erased
every trace of polytheism.

The floor of the Kaaba was cleaned with perfumed water
from Zamzam using ceramic brooms while the four walls
were perfumed with a mixture of Zamzam and rose water. It
was then incensed with Oud, a sweet smelling wood. Many
pilgrims rushed to bless themselves with drops of the water
which was carried away in small buckets.

The black covering of the Kaaba is an impressive work of
art which is made up of 47 pieces, each 14 meters long and 95
cm wide, covering 650 square meters. It contains 670 kilo-
grams of pure silk and 150 kg. of gold and silver.

A senior executive of the Muslim World League (MWL)
chided Muslims for not really understanding the challenges
facing Islam today. Muslim nations have to bring back the
principles and norms of Islam to the forefront. The religion has
to be tapped in a proper fashion to bring back the "golden ages."
Islam has much to offer in the challenging new world order; with
the fall of the communist ideology and disgruntlement with the
capitalist system.

No special status is accorded to any human being other
than Prophet Muhammad, Allahs messenger who has conveyed to mankind the last divine message.

Because life is man's most valuable asset and is designed for noble purposes, Islam has shown man the way to live it properly and enjoyably. Among the measures taken in this respect is inhibition of gambling which is really more tension-accelerating than tension-reducing. It is a grave abuse of life to make it subject to luck and mere chance. It is a deviation from the normal course of life, if one entrusts his lot to the mad wheel of games, and invests his abilities in the most unpredictable moves on a gambling table. To protect man from all these unnecessary mental strains and shattering nerves, and to enable him to lead a normal life in means as well as in ends, Islam has forbidden gambling of all forms and kinds.

People are classified into three groups: believers, nonbelievers, and hypocrites. The hypocrites ally themselves in practice with those who are hostile to Islam just as the hypocrites in Madinah at the time of the Prophet maintained close relations with the Jews. Thus, their evil ways are not limited to telling lies, deception, folly and making claims. They actually conspire with the enemies of Islam in a wicked and ignoble manner.

An information drive launched by the Muslim World League (MWL) office in Trinidad and Tobago succeeded in refuting the false propaganda carried out by the enemies of Islam.

Film producers in Turkey have increasingly turned their attention to producing films in various aspects of the Islamic religion, culture and civilization. Producer Mosod

Ogaqan has started work on film entitled "I am not alone brother." It deals with the subject matter of Muslim girl students at the Turkish Universities and the problems faced by them for their insistence on protecting their faith and wear veil at the campus .

One aspect of working for a living is what happens immediately after that joyous occasion known as "time to go home." In the United States, that often signals heading to a bar, restaurant or some social or cultural event. A reward for a job done, if not necessarily well done. This may contrast with the stereotypical view of the worker in the Islamic world, often seen today as living in an austere environment replete with religious observances of solemn behavior. Indeed, during the Gulf war there was concern that American troops stationed in Saudi Arabia might negatively influence the indigenous population with "Western" behavior unfit for Muslim consumption. In the early years of the development of Islam in the Mid-east, numerous cities sprang up and flourished in an atmosphere similar to those of today. But for a time, that atmosphere changed to one we would recognize in modern Western cities. Moreover, it was viewed as an acceptable way of life that complemented a deeply religious upbringing. Although a reversal from the more ascetic way of life to which Muslims had been accustomed, the "good life" continued through the 8th century exemplified by a woman named Seqainah, one of the heirs of the Prophet. Seqainah owned a salon peopled with poets intellectuals and politicians. With her, numerous husbands, she set a standard of carpe diem in marked contrast to the earlier, more conservative lifestyle.

When a man wants to contemplate over his position and wants to organize his religious thoughts, he runs away from the atmosphere of noise and uproar and takes shelter in a quiet place. And therefore if Islam recommends silence and considers it a means of civilized training, then it is not at all surprising. Undoubtedly the tongue is a rope in the hands of Satan. The faith of a man cannot be straight unless his heart is straight, and his heart cannot be straight unless his tongue becomes straight.

Islam cannot be learned from the actions of violent groups or political leaders who are torturing and killing Muslims. One should not judge the Qur'an when he has never read anything in it. Relying on the writings of the enemies of Islam is not an honest way of learning Islam. I also hope that the non-Muslims will be honest with themselves and not rely on the fake information about Muslims spread by Hollywood.

It is the collective duty of the Muslim community throughout the world to convey the message of Islam to mankind and to make it clear to everyone that Allah had chosen Islam as a faith and a code of living for the human race. Therefore, everyone is required by Allah to believe in the Oneness of Allah, the Supreme Being, and in the message of Prophet Muhammad (peace be on him). If there are impediments put in the way of the Muslim community to prevent it from discharging this duty, the community is expected to do everything in its power to remove these impediments.

The secretary of the Islamic centre in the Irish capital, Dublin, said Islam came to Ireland in 1957 with the arrival of a few Muslim students from South Africa. From this humble beginning the number of Muslim families in various parts of the country increased to 40 or 50 within a short while. Today the number of Muslims residing in Ireland has reached three thousand, most of them students.

If one carefully compares the early Islamic personality to the modern Islamic personality, the aspects of malformation in the latter will become clear. The major symptoms of this malformation are the following:
1. Weak Piety.
2. Being Influenced by Worldly Interests.
3. Fear of Life and Living.

Renowned Islamic scholar Sheikh Ahmed Deedat is the chairman of the Islamic Propagation Centre International. Sheikh Deedat is an authority on Holy Quran and the Bible. He is known all over the world for conducting debates with Christian missionaries with a view to remove misunderstandings about Islam and its beliefs. He has publicly debated with Jimmy Swaggert of the USA.

"Kashmir is not just the cause of its people. It is the cause of everyone who believes in Islam and the unity of God", Dr. Al-Quaid, assistant secretary-general of the World Assembly of Muslim Youth (WAMY), said here last night. The WAMY executive noted that Muslim struggle in Kashmir or elsewhere could succeed only if the Muslims imbibe the true spirit of jihad. He said that as long as the Muslims waged jihad, they remained strong and vibrant. Their decline began when they opted for soft options and easy living. The Islamic movement, he pointed out, had a strong mooring which neither the Indian rhetoric of secularism and socialism nor the degree of bawdy films and literature could shake off. "Liquor bars have disappeared. No obscene films are being shown. Women are wearing veil. And there is a growing attendance at mosques and Islamic schools."

All that Islam requires of non-Muslims generally is the right to address people in a free atmosphere. A Muslim minority in an overwhelmingly non-Muslim country should always try to maintain a peaceful relationship with the majority population, as indeed it is the case with a Muslim majority in a country which includes non-Muslim minorities.

What is the verdict on one who ridicules Islam? What is the ruling if he is an ignorant person? Any person who ridicules Islam is considered an infidel. But if he genuinely turns to God in repentance He will forgive him. This is because Islam deletes whatever that preceded such an act. Such a person, after repenting, must perform Ghusl - washing of the whole body - like an infidel who embraces Islam for the first time. If he is an ignorant person he must genuinely repent, show regret for what he committed, stop it completely and resolve not to repeat it.

Ulema differ on the issue of photographic pictures. Some consider them forbidden on the basis of numerous hadith by the Prophet (pbuh) and verses whose rulings are generalized while others say they are permissible because they are not hand-drawn pictures which is what is prohibited.

Islam is based on purification. Women do not pray or fast several days every month because of their menstruation. Cleanliness - physically as well as spiritually - is essential for communication with Almighty God. A Muslim must be clean, tidy and well-dressed. When a person embraces Islam, he should wash his whole body. Washing is also necessary before Friday congregational prayers and after sexual intercourse. The Prophet (pbuh) said that "purification is a half of the faith".

Most jurists concur that circumcision is an obligation, and not as our Muslim brother, Cyril Glasse, claimed in the Concise Encyclopaedia of Islam, that it is a tradition. Accordingly we follow Abraham (pbuh) in compliance with the Quranic verse, "Follow the religion of Abraham." However if a new Muslim cannot endure the pain of circumcision, it could be overlooked.

The adjective "kafer" is the Arabic term which denotes a non-believer. If you use the same word as a term of abuse, hurling it at a non-believer, you must have a good reason for that. If there is none, then you are wrong to call him by such a term, because it is bound to increase his antagonism to Islam and Muslims. Islam encourages us to deal kindly and fairly with non-Muslims as long as they do not start us with hostility. If they wish to be on friendly terms with us, then we must be friendly to them. To call someone a "kafer" although he may be one, is not conducive to good relations with other communities. Therefore, one must avoid it as much as one can.

Those known enemies of Islam, particularly the Zionist owned press, categorize every act directed to the supremacy of Islam as "fundamentalism", and its protagonists as "fundamentalists." Normally, it would be an honour to be called an Islamic fundamentalists for it denotes adherence to the fundamental principles of Islam. But, within this context, fundamentalism has become a word of scorn. The other side of the coin, however, has its positive dimension as well. For the first time in history the proceedings of the Congress in the United States is being opened with a Muslim prayer said by an American Muslim leader. This is what one can call the positive side of the Gulf war.

A friend of mine has pointed out to me that the Arabic number 18 is seen on the right palm of human beings, while the lines of the left palm make up the number 81. He suggests that we see in this an evidence of Allah's creation, since the combined numbers of what is written on both palms is 99 which corresponds to the number of Allah's names.

"We have too many mosques. It is becoming really funny. What we need are schools." Iranian Foreign Ministry senior analyst Hooshmand Mirfakhraei on life in Iran since 1979 Revolution.

Newsweek , June 10, 1991

There is no disagreement among scholars that apostasy or the reverting to some other religious beliefs after one has been a Muslim, is a grievous offense. Quite a substantial number of scholars are of the view that apostasy is a crime for which a specific punishment has been prescribed, and that punishment is death.

The Kashmir secessionist movement is by no means limited to the endeavors of gun-toting men and boys. With religion as their anchor the "Daughters of the Nation" — the Islamic Nation — provides various unarmed support services for the movement. Andhrebi, still in her twenties and a recent bride, serves as an inspirational force for the Muslim women of Kashmir. A Kashmir native, Andhrebi spent some time of her younger years in Canada, but returned to the valley and decided Western lifestyle was no substitute for "a better life based on the rules and principles of Islam." Andhrebi said although opinions concerning Kashmir's future differ throughout the valley "according to the principles of Islam, we must join Pakistan. Islam says Muslims should not be divided into nations. Accession to Pakistan is only the first step on the ladder to uniting Muslims and eventually instituting God's government worldwide", she said. "But before we can go to the superpowers and impose Islamic rule over there, I have just one capability. I can do it in Kashmir."

Press reports said Muslims in Brazil were in need of building an Islamic Centre and schools for teaching the Islamic religion and Arabic language. As the number of Muslims was constantly growing, the report said, the need for more Islamic schools and centres was becoming more and more pressing. The report added that despite the presence of a large number of Jews and their manipulations the Muslims were bravely protecting their faith and culture.

There are two main references in the Qur'an to the jinn. What we know of the jinn is that they are creatures of Allah whom we cannot see, although they see us. They share the planet earth with us and they live in nations and communities. They are required to believe in Islam in the same way as we do. We are also told in the Qur'an that the majority of them are disbelievers, just like human beings. This means that they are susceptible to faith like us, but they have temptations which divert their path away from it.

Examples of cruelty to animals are numerous - Muslim and Jewish slaughter methods are certainly not among them. To falsely accuse Muslim and Jewish slaughter methods of being "barbaric" is nothing less than "cruelty" to Muslims and Jews, as it certainly stirs up misguided racial hatred and religious intolerance. Contrary to popular Western belief, the spirit of Islam is mercy and Islam stresses the importance of treating all animals kindly. The Prophet Muhammad (pbuh) told the story of a harlot who, on seeing a thirsty dog, went down to a well and filled her shoes with water for the dog to drink - an act of compassion that earned her God's forgiveness for all her sins and earned her a place in paradise.

There is nothing in Islam which need be taken blindly. Every precept and every principle of faith has a particular purpose behind it. If we understand these principles, our faith is likely to be stronger. We should not hesitate to inquire.

Islam lays special emphasis on the appearance of a Muslim who is required to take care of himself and his clothes. He should maintain both his body and clothes clean. What he wears should fit with the Islamic ethical standards and should not invite bad comments. To wear a shirt carrying a picture of a pop star is indicative of the wearer's petty concerns. Hence, it is discouraged or reprehensible.

The American troops seemed to be hungry to learn about Islam. "Thee Americans loved it." Many modern-day Christians, including the bishops of the Anglican Church, do not believe in the miraculous birth of Jesus (pbuh), and his being a savior. Deedat (see page 22) emphasized that he wanted 10 Saudi volunteers to help him distribute books about Jesus in Islam, half a million each on the streets of New York, Los Angeles, Chicago, Salt Lake City, with a happy new year greeting.

More than 6,000 people gathered at the Dayton, Ohio Convention Center for an Islamic meeting. They represent one of the fastest-growing religious groups in the United States and Canada. But they feel misunderstood. Though Islam is said to be the fastest-growing faith in the world, exact figures on the Muslim population in the United States are elusive because there is no official count. The Census Bureau does not ask questions on religious affiliation. The lack of information frustrates many Muslims, who say it contributes to the stereo-types of them and their faith. African-Americans see Islam as an alternative to a system that is incapable of accepting and absorbing them. A major issue was the question of coexisting with the broader society, or being assimilated into it. Integration may remain elusive, particularly for women.

Many of the US soldiers who returned from Saudi Arabia now possess a profound understanding and respect for Islam as a comprehensive way of life. It is no longer that stereo-type of the past. Islam has finally come home to the US.

The demographer Ben Wattenberg writes that the United States can now be truly called a melting pot because for the first time it includes a significant number of Muslims. The Islam Society of North America has put great emphasis on traditions and customs, but that Islam should not be viewed as dress and diet only. "My grandparents converted to Islam," said Janet Rasheeda Bryant, "and frankly I think it was because it was not white but also because it doesn't tell you what to do. It says it is better for you to do certain things, but it doesn't dictate. It's a very gentle religion."

A new Islamic welfare society has been formed in Jeddah. The society collects surplus food from banquets of wedding halls and other parties for distribution to needy people. It also collects torn religious books and that contain portions of the Quran and Hadith and disposes of them properly.

What we have to understand is that Islam preaches tolerance. Over the centuries, Muslims all over the world have
shown a degree of religious tolerance which can hardly be
equalled by other religions. If a dispute is likely to generate
strife and troubles, then Islam would do everything possible to
prevent it, even if that leads to giving the other party some
privileges to which they are not entitled. Islam is not a faith which
seeks the suppression of other religions, nor does it stamp out
religious freedom.

Presently, Muslim minority communities in several countries are faced with a very critical situation. Generally speaking, due to the rise of religious and ethnic consciousness
among a majority of the people of the world, particularly in
under developed and developing countries, a certain latent
hostility and distrust are to be found almost everywhere. So in
the ultimate sense it is no longer a matter of one or two
countries where survival and continued existence of Muslim
minorities is threatened, the phenomenon is universal. It is
also unprecedented in its dimensions. The world community
has not experienced anything like this before.

With regard to the external domain, the general cliche that
all Muslim minorities everywhere, are subject in all aspects
of their lives to discrimination and persecution is no longer
tenable. What is needed is a specific study of each minority
country or cluster of countries like Muslims under communism, Muslims living with Catholics in Latin America with
Protestants in Europe, with Hindus in India, Buddhists in Sri
Lanka, animists and racists in Africa etc.

According to the Korea Muslim Federation, there are about 32,000 registered Korean Muslims nationwide. Three Koreans are currently studying to be Muslims. Islam was first introduced to Korea by Turkish soldiers who were fighting with the United Nations forces during the 1950-53 Korean War. "A lot of Koreans are reluctant to become Muslims because drinking is prohibited and one must pray five times a day wherever they are, which they think is a cumbersome thing to do for busy Koreans."

The Islamic world would soon be watching the one-hour Islamic television program transmitted through Scula satellite from Boston in the USA. The program would include recitation from the Holy Quran and news of the world from the point of view of the Islamic world. Coverage of Islamic events is arranged through the Voice of the Arab World television in Boston.

The lack of required qualifications in most of the employees of the Organization for the Promotion of Virtue and Prevention of Vice has resulted in some of them behaving in an unacceptable manner. The director of the Organization said they did not receive the kind of attention the other agencies dealing with justice or education have got. A person who is dealing with guidance (religious rulings) should be either a Ph.D. holder or have the qualifications of a judge. There are 5,000 people working for the organization which has 450 centres spread over the Kingdom. The main function of the organization is to publicly announce the prevention of vice. The objective of the organization is to reform the behavior and manner of the Muslim community in the light of Sharia.

The Academy of Islamic Studies, a Muslim school which serves the Islamic community in Minnesota may be forced to close its doors unless financial assistance is received quickly. The academy is the only full-time Islamic school available to the Muslim community in the state of Minnesota. Without the opportunity to attend an Islamic school, Muslim students will be forced to enter the American public schools system where peer pressure and stereotypes of Muslims make many young people turn away from Islamic values. The United States Internal revenue Service is now demanding payment of almost $8,000 they say the academy owes in taxes. '

The Muslim community in Montreal, Canada, has undertaken a project for construction of a complex in the city centre, named after the historic Muslim city of Kairouan, comprising a mosque and an Islamic institute. Community leaders said the project would cost $400,000, but so far only $25,000 had been collected. Sheikh Sunno has contribution to building on many mosques in North America.

We often say that the sort of free mixing that prevailed in past generations in Europe has led to the sort of permissiveness that we now witness. In some parts of the Muslim world, the extended family provides a chance of free mixing which is not much different from what was known in Europe in the last century. This is something that Islam does not approve. Countering it is best achieved through Islamic learning.

The important point about disposing of newspapers and waste paper with Qur'anic verses is that there should be no element of disrespect in the way you dispose of them. Thus, such wastepaper should not be thrown on the dump heap if the practices in your area are such that would make the paper bearing Qur'anic verses or the name of Allah liable to be treaded upon or used with total disregard to what it contains. The best thing perhaps is to burn such papers. If that is not easy to do, then perhaps you could cut out the Qur'anic verses or the phrase you have mentioned and tear it into small pieces so that the Qur'anic verses is no longer identifiable.

An English encyclopedia contains serious errors in its presentation on Islam, while the entry on Spain almost whitewashes the Arab contribution to its civilization and culture. The entry on Islam on Page 130 describes Islam as "A monotheistic religion founded by Muhammad (570-632) in the first half of the 7th century A.D." In the next paragraph: "Islam represented in one sense the reaction of some of the arab elite of the city-oasis against, the antiquated tribal structure of Arabia whose religion was eclectic, muddled, and feeble." Another serious mistake occurs on Page 134 on the subject of Prophet Abrahams willingness to sacrifice his son. The reference, which is made in the context of the submissive attitude of a Muslim in relation to Allah, reads: "submission and fatalism become strong characteristics of the followers of Islam, and the example of Abraham and his willingness to sacrifice Isaac became the archetype for submission to the will of God."

The Muslim population of the United States is growing with one American embracing Islam a day. The

American Muslim Council in Washington D.C. predicted
that by the year 2000 Muslims will be the second largest faith
after Christianity in the US. They said that of the more than
250 million population of the US, around 5 million to 6 million
are Muslims although the exact number could not be determined
after the entry on faith and religion in the census was scratched
in 1957 on instigation of the Jewish lobby. The AMC said that
by 1992, a million Muslim voters will troop to the polls and
enhance the number of Muslims occupying top positions in
various local, educational, county, state and federal bodies.
The only ranking Muslim officials in the US now are two of
the more than 14,000 legislative aides in the House of Representatives, the deputy mayor of Detroit and a drug enforcement
executive in Nevada. The small number of Muslims holding
public offices is due to "our own failure." There are also a few
Muslims in the fields of science and technology, but they shy
away from the limelight as they are intimated by the Jewish
lobby. The recitation of the Holy Quran at the opening of the
House of Representatives is one of the achievements of the
AMC.

There is no harm in two Muslim countries starting the
month of Ramadan, or indeed any other month on two different
days. The use of telescopes and other equipment to determine
the appearance of the moon is permissible and may be acted
upon. This, however, would not resolve the problem, because
the new moon may be visible in one area but not in a
neighboring area.

According to one survey of Christian religion in
America, "forty one percent American Christians believe

their religion is not concerned enough with social issues." In the West the problems with parents in their old age is becoming a big issue. Parents usually don't take more responsibilities of their children as they want to save money for their old age when they will have to live in isolation or in old age homes. They need their savings for those days. Every problem has a solution. In Muslim societies there is neither the concept of old age homes nor the modern "institution" of babysitters. Usually parents live with their children and all grandchildren are brought up by grandparents. They are helpful to each other. When their sons get older and can't serve their parents, grandchildren take care of their grandparents.

It is not right to describe everything in Western society as bad and everything in Eastern society as good. What we can properly say is that in a proper Islamic society, things are all good, as long as they conform to Islamic teachings.

The Muslim World League, an international Islamic nongovernment organization founded 30 years ago by a distinguished gathering of Islamic scholars in Makkah to remove the weakness and disarray from the Muslim ranks, is playing an important role in imparting Islamic education to Muslim children. The objective of the MWL is to establish "the Muslim teaching as the dominating one in the whole world and thus create an order based on Islamic principles". The need for Islamization of education was first investigated in the 1977 conference in Mekkah in view of the secularist basis of modern education. The task is mind-boggling. Nearly two centuries of neglect and backwardness has created a backlog which must be cleared before any appreciable progress can be made. The MWL

hopes that other organizations will come forward to join the
MWL in this Jihad against the combined forces of ignorance,
polytheism and kufr.

About 3,000 soldiers from various countries which participated in the Gulf war last year, embraced Islam, said the
head of the Islamic Call Committee at the World Assembly of
Muslim Youth (WAMY). WAMY noted that a lot of non-
Muslims have embraced Islam following the collapse of
materialistic ideologies and their failure to solve the problems
of the mankind. It was noted that the Saudi society which is
characterized by adherence to Islam gives a good example for
the Islamic society .

With a community of three million, Islam is the second
biggest religion in France after Catholicism. Paradoxically,
the law of the separation of the church and the state, that is to
say the principle of secularism, allows the Muslim religion to
develop freely in France. The Muslim community is a vast
mosaic of nationalities and ethnic groups, but also of dogmas
and rites, although the Sunnis form the large majority. However, it offers its members an increasingly assorted cultural
and moral reference. With the opening of religious centres,
bookshops and shops for halal meat, the presence of Islam can
be seen in daily life. School dinners and staff canteens offer
alternatives to food forbidden by Islam. But the diversity
within this community is detrimental to its cohesion. The
variety in the national origins reproduces the political differences which sometimes oppose the states, not to mention the
problems of cohabitation between Algerians and the
repatriate Muslims from Algeria. The 800 associations which

cater to most of the Islamic trends were unable to agree on electing a representative for the French state.

Freedom from communism does not imply, as some people would have us believe, that the alternative is the way of live which prevails in that part of the world commonly referred to as the "civilized world". The very nature of the people of these Central Asian republics are indications that they belong to the true civilization; Islam. As such it is therefore the duty of the Muslim world at large to come to the assistance of these victims of the red ideology.

When the famous Black American, Malcolm X, who at one time led the black nationalist movement against the whites, performed Haj after embracing Islam, he saw people of all races, colours, and nationalities converging on the same place - Arafat - with the same appearance, wearing the same Ihram, chanting the same words: Labaik Allahummah Labaik.

The rise of Islam is perhaps the most amazing event in human history. Springing from a land and a people like previously negligible, Islam spread within a century over half the earth, shattering great empires, overthrowing long-established religions, remoulding the souls of races and building up a whole new world order - the world of Islam. Arising in a desert land sparsely inhabited by a nomad race previously undistinguished in human annals. Islam sallied forth on its great adventure with the slenderest human backing and against the heaviest material odds.

Yet Islam triumphed with seemingly miraculous ease, and a couple of generations saw the fiery crescent borne victorious from the Pyrenees to the Himalayas and from the deserts of Central Africa .

Islam is probably the religion most misunderstood by people in different parts of the world and if those people have the opportunity to know Islam well, they can't help being it's followers. Islam is the last and most comprehensive message from God to all mankind. In fact, it is the only way to salvation.

In the Prophet's words we are, by divine right, the leaders of mankind. But here, instead of taking this broad field of humanity we have made our little ghettos and say no, no, a Muslim first and man later. A Muslim should be God's first creature who should say man and then Muslim. Now the irony is that the people of other faiths are saying man first and then Christians or Jews or whatever later. If we are serious about it, this is the time to start

Cairo, Oct 9 (R) - Former heavyweight boxing champion Muhammad Ali left Egypt yesterday vowing to set up an Islamic lobby in the United States to fight the influence of the Zionist lobby. "President Mubarak has promised to help found the powerful Islamic lobby to combat the Zionist lobby in the United States," Ali said in a statement at Cairo airport. Ali, 44, met Mubarak during two weeks spent in Egypt as a guest of honor at the African Games. He left Cairo for Damascus, where he said he would discuss the lobby idea with Syrian officials. Ali said

Cairo's prestigious Al-Ayhar University had promised to send teachers to Islamic schools he planned to set up in the United States.

PSYCHOLOGISTS, and others who try to quantify feelings paint this picture of the 'typical' person living in America: He or she places personal desire before the needs of society; is more likely to feel isolation than companionship; will usually not directly intervene in the lives of others, even to bring about good; has or will experience the disunion of his immediate family; is likely to have lived through the dissolution of neighborhood and feel unsafe; likely to express doubt about ethical standards of his collegial, professional, or vocational environment; feel both helpless before government and a widening gap between himself and his leaders; and tends to be pessimistic about goodness of human beings and the direction humanity is headed. Such devastating anti-social expressions beset any nation that shirks the laws that Allah and His Prophet have laid down as "Obligations of the Heart." Among them is ukhuwwa, or brotherhood, perhaps the best bulwark against the skittish feelings and fatal social diseases mentioned here. Ukhawwa is the basic social contract that every Muslim enters into with every other as part of his or her commitment to Islam. It is the glue that holds a society together and is regarded as integral to the Shariah. Ultimately, it is the difference between social disarray and nationhood.

Shaikh Rashid Ahmed, Pakistan's minister for cultural affairs, issued an invitation this week to Madonna and Jackson to share the stage in an entertainment extravaganza tentatively set for February. There was no immediate response. "We want to show the world that we are not a country of militant fundamentalists. We are an open society We want a new image for the people of Pakistan." The religious party Jamaat-e-Islami has other ideas. Jamaat is threatening to take to the streets again if Madonna and Jackson bring their glittery shows to Pakistan.

FINANCE

A study has been published in the US on the concept of Islamic financial establishments with the aim of making Muslims attain their economic aspirations through the viable financial organizations. There are two Islamic associations in the US founded on a combined sum of $9 Million. The lack of sufficient capital was the cause of their ineffectiveness although there were other factors that lead to the poor functioning of the banks. Some of these factors included ignorance of Islamic laws among the Muslim community and their inability to apply the *Shariah* law on financial transactions in the US. Poor performance of the Islamic banking system is attributed to the inability of the Muslim community to convince the international Western banking organizations of the justness and equitable potential performance of the Islamic banking system. One further factor was that some wealthy people were prone to invest their money in dubious business ventures purely out of the desire to make a quick profit.

Islam and banks are on two opposite poles. Western governments enter into schemes that unrealistically superimpose Western-industrial values onto cultures not geared for such systems. With astronomical interest rates, a vicious circle of re-scheduled debts and further loans drag the countries into the Western economic mud. In Islam there is no such thing as banking as *riba* is prohibited. The main instrument for re-distribution of wealth is *zakaah*.

The existing economic system is based on the principle of *riba* and basic enrichment of a few at the expense of the majority. Islam has achieved the exact opposite. It has to create the broadest possible prosperity in a society. People with money would distribute to a *waof* trust which would use the funds for social upliftment.

All investment contracts must be approved by the Religious Supervisory Board to ensure they conform to the requirements of the *Shariah*. This board consists of six Islamic scholars

It is clear that the followers of two different religions may not inherit each other.

Incurring a debt is not something that Islam encourages, even when the reason for it is to perform a religious duty.

Islamic nations must put an end to economic dependents and become self reliant through mutual cooperation. "Dependence translates into an erosion of sovereignty. In material terms it means becoming vulnerable to blatant exploitation." Though the Islamic states were rich in manpower and natural resources, most were bracketed in the low and middle income categories.

We have a very clear-cut ruling on usury which cannot be disputed by anyone: "Allah has made trade lawful and has forbidden usury." The question remains whether interest is usury. There is no doubt that both have some aspects in common which tend to strongly associate interest with usury. But there are also some aspects which the two transactions differ. When you deposit your money in a bank, you are not lending it to the bank. Moreover, the money remains available to you all the time, etc. Nevertheless interest-based banking is central to the capital economic system which is usurious in nature. Therefore, we continue to say that interest is forbidden to take or to give. A Muslim must not have anything to do with interest whenever that is possible.

The Pakistani President yesterday urged the Islamic world to build its own financial institutions with a view to achieving financial security and self-reliance in economic development. "This was a prerequisite for meaningful self-reliance and would also lead to closer unity and durable collaboration among the Muslim countries."

A United Arab Emirates business leader says the closure of the Bank of Credit and Commerce International (BCCI) is a Western plot to weaken Arab banks. "The conspiracy against BCCI was not the first and will not be the last so long as the Arab banking sector lacks solidarity in the international arena. The business man said that certain Western capitals had masterminded a conspiracy.

Some car dealers sell a car with a down payment and the rest of the price in installments. The seller then charges a higher price for the car sold. Is this practice permissible under Sharia? This type of business deals are permissible. Since the deal is according to economic morals, there is no harm, according to the Sharia, in finalizing it.

Growing debts in non-oil Arab states are hindering economic growth, discouraging investors and threatening the shift to market economy, regional experts said. The burden of debt servicing on available resources poses a serious threat to the Arab countries which need foreign financing to support reform programs. It also dissuades the return of capital from abroad and foreign investment and undermine the credibility of reforms. Several Arab countries have sought to privatize their state-controlled economy as a solution to their chronic economic hardship. But the pace of reforms has been slow, mainly because of the lack of funds and the absence of a privatization strategy.

The Saudi Investment Bank has extended 268,818 loans worth over SR3.7 billion since its inception 19 years ago until the end of 1990. The bank extends loans to enable Saudis get married, start small businesses, seek medical treatment or renovate houses. Marriage loans accounted for 55.7% of the total number of loans. The repayment rate for the loans has so far exceeded 98%.

A Muslim should have nothing to do with interest. Sometimes, however, people find themselves with interest paid to them and they do not know what they should or can do with it. The first thing to remember is that they must not leave it to the bank, particularly if the bank happens to be in a non-Muslim country. The bank is then obliged, in most cases, to donate the money to some charitable organizations, some of which may indeed be hostile to Islam. In this way a Muslim supports an organization which is hostile to his faith This is absurd.

Equality and fair share occur in relation to permissible things and also in relation to things unlawful. Injustice is the consequence when there is a monopolizing of things in the permissible category, such as food, drink, marriage, clothing, transport and goods. The root of stinginess and envy is greed. Envy contains within it both stinginess and injustice, since it is stingy in respect of what others have given, and unjust in seeking to deprive them of it. Creation of monopolies lead to sin. It should therefore be avoided at all cost.

Capitalism today is confronted with a crisis whose meaning and significance are not fully comprehended by it. The new concept of the emerging new world order is a manifestation of the failure of pure capitalism. Islam's difference with capitalism is that Islam stands for free enterprise, and appears theoretically capable of working it out without the necessity of having to face the contradictory dilemmas of capitalism. This is on account of Islam's uncompromising hostility to the institution of interest. Islam differs from capitalism in its rejection of interest as the basis of credit and in its consequent ability to sustain free enterprise without finding itself confronted with the contradictions which have barred the path of development of man. The difference between the two in one sentence can be stated thus: while both claim to support free enterprise, objective reality does not prove the claim of capitalism; and its future projections are likely to whittle down whatever is left. Islam's capacity to sustain free enterprise, in spite of its theoretically positivist stance in the face of the challenges of today, is still struggling to externalize itself as an objective reality.

If you wish to make use of the services provided by banks, keep in mind that any interest given on deposits used for lending is unlawful to have. If you give instructions to the bank to invest your money in a lawful way, as in a profit and-loss-sharing account, then the money you receive on your investment is perfectly legitimate.

The United Saudi Commercial Bank has announced SR126.6 million profits as of September this year. Despite declining interest rates scenario both at domestic and international scene the bank managed to maintain the growth in its operating income. The sizeable increase in loans and advances indicates the bank's commitment to   meet domestic credit requirements.

CHARITY

In response to world disasters the Muslim as an individual remains complacent, and non-responsive at the whole episode of human tragedy. We have second thoughts, "as long as the inferno and suffering does not touch me, it's allright." This complacent attitude has led the Muslims into a corner of distrust, dishonor and ridicule.

The yardstick of per capita income, and per capita public spending on social services are inadequate in an Islamic society, since they lack the spiritual and religious content of welfare. This can be explained by quoting an example from the life of the Prophet (pbuh) when a women came to him and said: "I get fits of epilepsy and my body becomes uncovered. Please invoke Allah for me." The Prophet said: "If you wish, You can be patient and enter Paradise, and if you wish, I will invoke Allah and cure you" She said: "I will remain patient," and added, "but I become uncovered, so please invoke for me that I may not become uncovered". So he invoked Allah for her.

If worldwide statistics were available of the amount given away by Muslims as charity throughout the month of Ramadan or used in charitable projects like homes for orphans, the destitute, etc; the figures would be astounding. The reason Muslims become more open-handed in Ramadan is because they want to add as much as possible to their good deeds of fasting, praying, and all that is enjoined.

In charity dinners, people compete for the limelight and the interest generated by larger and larger contributions. There is thus the marked element of pride involved. Islam is keen to stamp it out from all charitable actions.

HEAVEN AND HELL

Believers will cross "the bridge to hell" as quickly as a wink, or lightening, or wind, or fast horses. What determines their speed is the quality of their deeds in this world. Those with the best deeds are the first to cross it. The last of them to cross the bridge to hell is a man who has no more light than the size of his large toe, and who stumbles over the bridge. It is needless to say that the nonbelievers will not be able to cross the bridge and will fall into hell.

It is part of the basic Islamic beliefs that after resurrection, we will account for our deeds and we will be judged accordingly. Angels are sent to people in their graves to question them about their beliefs. He is sat up and asked about his view of the Prophet. For the non believers the grave is made so narrow for him that his ribs crack. All this applies to people who are buried, cremated, drowned or eaten up by wild beasts.

A very important point about drawing up Wills is that it may not be made according to our whims. We are not to have favorites. In terms of the Holy Qu'ran, justice should be the spirit of the Will. We may not disinherit the rightful heirs.

A Muslim should shudder at the Qu'ranic injunction that warns us that if we do not follow the order of making Wills properly we shall suffer in Hell; the most miserable state for any soul to be in.

From the Hadith we get the following:

1. The angels are created from "light" and are invisible.

2. They do not have any free will or an independent will to act on their own.

3. They carry out without question all the commands (laws) of Allah and do not oppose or neglect them in any way.

4. Like everything in the universe, day and night they are engaged in praising and glorifying Allah and are never tired of this.

5. They carry out their functions honestly, efficiently and responsibly, and are never guilty of shirking work.

6. The number of angels is only known to Allah, however four of them are well known: Gabriel, Israfil, Michael, and Izrail.

7. Two angels, called 'Munkar' and 'Nakir' are sent to the graves to question a person after his/her death.

The four angels can be explained in terms of the four forces that exist in nature. These four obey the laws of Allah incessantly without any mistakes, without any disobedience. These four forces are the Gravitational Force, Electromagnetic Force, Weak Force, and the Strong Force, or Nuclear Force.

Heaven may be likened to a big garden or a palace with many doors. A person who wants to get into that garden or that palace may enter through any of these doors. Once he has entered, he is already in. He should not worry too much over which door he got through. The most important thing is that he gets in. Heaven has so many doors: One of them is pilgrimage, another is charity, a third is jihad, a fourth is fasting, a fifth is night worship, etc. A person who manages to get admitted into heaven scores a great success. Whether he does it through pilgrimage, jihad, or generous charity is of no consequence.

Two angels are assigned to each of us and they record everything that we do. May I tell you that I do not know the nature of these records. They are certainly more than a simple description of the actions we do. The records may be in the form of a book supported by a video which shows every action of ours and how it was done.

⊙

There are very convincing reasons to believe in life after death. Firstly, all the prophets have called their people to believe in life after death. Secondly, whenever a human society is built on the basis of this belief, it has been most ideal and peaceful society free of social and moral evils. Thirdly, history bears witness that whenever this belief is rejected collectively by a group of people in spite of the repeated warning of the prophet, the group as a whole has been punished by God even in this world. Fourthly, moral, aesthetic and rational faculties of man endorse the possibility of life after death. Fifthly, God's attributes of Justice and Mercy have no meaning if there is no life after death.

LAW AND ORDER

So often the non-Muslim world look at punishment being meted out in public as cruel. What's more appropriate; having sympathy for the victim of the crime, or with the criminal? You will no doubt say, "with the victim" This is precisely what happens in Muslim countries. This has the effect of scaring off potential criminals in a country such as Saudi Arabia. It is interesting to note that when it was announced at a soccer match in Bulgaria that those who misbehaved will be tried in public on the spot, the match proceeded with no incident of crime taking place.

The following notices were taken from newspaper articles as they occurred in an Islamic country. The notice of execution comes only after the execution has taken place in public. The newspapers never carry the stories of the crimes when they happen. Execution is done buy chopping the head from the body before the public.

May 24, 1991 - murderer who killed six people was executed today.

May 31, 1991 - Eight people were executed today after being convicted of various crimes in different cases. Offenses included drug trafficking, sexual assault, robbery and murder.

June 7, 1991 - Seven people including a first lieutenant and a corporal were executed today in different convictions of drug trafficking, sexual assault, robbery and murder.

July 19, 1991 - The Ministry of Interior announced that a man convicted of cold-blooded murder was executed in Sharorah today. A statement by the Ministry said AL Hamdi had shot and killed Al Harithy in revenge for slapping his brother on the face in front of a group of friends. While making this public, the Ministry would like to stress the government's determination to maintain peace and order and deal harshly with criminals who try to disturb the peace and security.

There are a few offenses for which Islam prescribes a particular punishment, such as theft, waging war against the Muslim state, unsubstantiated accusations of adultery, and adultery. Each one of these offenses has specified punishment which must be inflicted once the offense has been proven in accordance with Islamic legal requirements or admitted by the offender. The punishment of such offenses have three distinctive features: 1) they must be inflicted in the public interest, 2) they can be neither increased nor reduced, 3) the offender cannot be pardoned either by the victim, the judge considering the case or indeed the head of the state.

July 27, 1991: Two people were executed here today after being convicted of shooting a couple to death, according to a statement issued by the Interior Ministry. The men broke into the house with the intention of rape. The wife suddenly woke up frightened and awakened her husband. One man fatally shot the couple leaving the baby drenched in the blood of his parents, while the other stood guard. The capital punishment pronounced by the Shariah Court was duly endorsed by the Court of Cassation and the Supreme Judiciary Council and subsequently royal order for execution was issued, the statement said.

2 August 1991 - Three men were executed here this morning for robbery and rape. A statement from the ministry said the three broke into a house in broad daylight during last Ramadan (March/April 1991) after making sure that the owner had left. They entered the room where the man's wife was sleeping threatened her with a knife, stole her jewelry and raped her. The men fled in a car, but security authorities caught them. They were found by the local Sharia court guilty of the crime and sentenced to death. The verdict was upheld by the Court of Cassation, Supreme Judicial Board. The ministry warned that a similar fate awaits those who would commit such crimes.

2 August 1991- A man was executed here today for trying to sexually assault a woman and for previous similar crimes. The man drove his car towards a woman who was attending to a herd of sheep and asked her to have sex with him. When the woman refused, he beat her up, forced her into the car and drove away. The woman fainted and he dropped her in an isolated place thinking she was dead. After the man was arrested he was found to have committed similar crimes. In fact he is feared in his place.

3 August 1991 - Pakistan said yesterday it would impose the death penalty on anyone making a disrespectful or derogatory remark about the Prophet Muhammad. The country's penal code formally stipulated life imprisonment for offenses against the Prophet. "Now, after amending the law, an accused guilty of committing disrespect or use of derogatory remarks in respect of the Holy Prophet will face only the death sentence and there will be no alternate punishment."

MANILA, Aug. 1 (R) - A grenade exploded in front of a mosque and killed two Muslims, including a cousin of a former Philippine ambassador to Saudi Arabia, police said. Five other Muslims were injured. The explosion occurred four days after a grenade blast, blamed by police on Muslims, killed two foreign Christian missionaries and injured 21 foreigners in Zamboanga City on the southern Philippine island of Mindanao.

Pakistan, which stands at the crossroads, can pull back from the brink only by implementing the Islamic Shariah which will ensure social and economic justice, (Dr. Muhammad Umer Chhapra). The root cause, he pointed out, was the lack of social and economic justice which bred frustration, leading to aggression. When wealth was cornered by the rich, jobs went out to the undeserving, and vote was cast for a consideration, they would promote a climate of frustration and violence, Dr. Chhapra said. He also underlined the need for educating the mothers in the interest of proper upbringing of the child, and regretted a poor showing on this front. Female literacy in Pakistan stood at 19 percent as against 30 percent for the national average. The yawning Gulf between the haves and have-nots could not be bridged by either communism or capitalism, both of which have failed. Only Islam could provide the solution for overcoming the problems. A nation's downfall begins when it becomes rotten to the core. Islam prevents this decay and is a factor for economic uplift.

Custodian of the Two Holy Mosques King Fahad has ordered that prisoners who memorize the Holy Quran or part of it should be eligible for commutation of their sentence. The order provides that the sentence of a prisoner who memorizes the entire Quran will be commuted by half. The prisoner who memorizes half of the holy book will have his sentence reduced by one fourth, and one who memorizes a quarter of the Quran will have his sentence reduced by one-eighth. The privilege, however, is extended only to prisoners whose sentence is not less than six months, the chapters memorized not less than two, and that only entire chapters will be taken into consideration. The general president of the Organization for Enjoining Virtue and Preventing Vice lauded the generosity of the royal decree. Some prisoners who were once beyond reform now try memorizing the Holy Quran. Once the light of the belief enters their hearts, they voluntarily give up their evil ways, the president said. The royal decree has caused an increase in the number of prisoners studying the Holy Quran.

"Those who do not observe the Islamic dress codes in Iran are not executed and what the Western media have attributed to me are pure lies," said Iran's Prosecutor General. The Prosecutor-General said that ignoring the dress code would be considered apostasy, punishable by death under Iran's Islamic laws. Hardcore followers demand that even women whose hair slips from under the covering be punished. A fight over attempts to detain women not consid- ered fully covered precipitated a riot in the central city of Isfahan last month. (Aug. 91)

One should avoid swearing in Allah's name as a habit unless there is a desperate necessity or if he is requested to do so by a judicial commission or a Sharia Court. Swearing in one's own creed or honour, or in the name of some other people or creature's or certain holy places, or even in the name of a Prophet, is a wrong practice which is more or less a kind of polytheism.

30 August 1991: A man was executed today after being convicted of kidnapping a boy and assaulting him sexually. The man accosted the boy in front of the latter's house and forced him into his car before driving off to a remote area where he committed the crime. It was proved that he commit- ted a similar crime earlier. The capital punishment pro- nounced by the Shariah Court was duly endorsed by the Court of Cassation and the Supreme Judiciary Council.

When a Muslim commits a sin, particularly one which is punishable by a specific punishment, he should not publicize what he has done. Publicity is an additional sin. If he makes a confession of what he had done, the punishment prescribed by Allah must be enforced. To make such a confession is permissible, but the person who commits a sin should not lift the mantle with which Allah has covered it. Therefore, a person who commits adultery should not publicize that. If he has a child born to him illegitimately and he marries the mother of the child, no one will ask him about the legitimacy of the child.

The relationship between the illegitimate child and his father is broken. This means that neither the child nor the father have any rights or duties toward each other. The two are like strangers. This means that the child does not have the right to be supported by the father, but equally the father cannot require the child to be dutiful to him.

Police in the Philippines arrested "several" suspected Muslim separatists on Monday in connection with a terrorists attack on a Protestant missionary group at the weekend which left the two foreign women dead. The attack on late Sunday came as some 100 members of the group were holding a farewell party aboard a ship.

Three drunks who burnt down a mosque in Northern France have been jailed for between six months and four years.

September 9, 1991: A Sudanese court ordered hands amputated from two men convicted of stealing food, an official newspaper reported today. The sentences are the first since such penalties were restored last March. The newspaper said the court in Sinnar, central Sudan, found the two men guilty of stealing wheat and sugar from a store.

Authors note: I was once told by an individual who had witnessed an amputation just how it was done. Blood flow to the hand is restricted by a tourniquet. The arm is restrained in one direction while the hand is stretched out in the other direction. A knife is used to cut the tendons at the wrist until the hand pops off.

New Delhi, India: A 60-year-old Saudi Arabian sheik appeared in court Sunday, a day after he was arrested for marrying a 10-year-old Indian girl and trying to take her home with him. A growing demand for young Indian Muslim brides has been reported in the Persian Gulf in recent years. Investigators said the sheik was suspected of being part of a slave-running gang.

18 Sept. 1991: A UAE court has sentenced a 14 year old boy in the UAE to 30 lashes with the whip for stealing money from his mother. The boy admitted stealing $790 from his mothers wardrobe to buy clothes and perfume. The judge was quoted as saying the verdict was necessary to deter the boy.

25 September 1991: A Pakistani court sentenced two American brothers today to the Islamic punishment of amputation of a hand and a foot for robbery. The two have a week in which to appeal against the sentence, which also included five to 10 years of hard labour before being deported, a court statement said. The two men were charged with robbing a bank of about $3,365 last June. The court found them guilty and "ordered the amputation

of their right hands from the wrist and left feet from the ankle," the court statement said.

2 October 1991: The United States has raised concerns with Pakistan about two American brothers who are appealing an Islamic Court sentence that they each have a hand and a foot amputated for robbing a bank. "We're very concerned about this case. This is a particularly harsh sentence. No American has ever been amputated in Pakistan for committing a crime." The brothers deny the charge, contending the trial judge ignored defence evidence.

16 October 1991: Two American brothers sentenced to have a hand and foot amputated for a bank robbery they denied committing were both cleared of all charges today. The appeals had been allowed because of a lack of evidence. The two brothers and their wives had moved to Pakistan in search of a "better Islamic environment". Neither of the wives conform to the strictest Islamic rules that women should be covered from head to toe.

RITUALS

When you go to bed you can follow the sunnah of the Prophet and cup your hands, put them to your mouth and blow air into them and then read the last three surahs then go with your hands all over your body. You repeat this three times, then you glorify Allah and praise Him.

Since sharing in sacrificing a cow is permissible for Pilgrims when the sacrifice is a duty, it is permissible for *aqeequh* which is a recommended practice. Sacrificing a cow for two boys is more than adequate.

Our religion is not a set of rituals. It is a constitution and a way of living. It has a very clear code of practice. If we want to be true Muslims, we have to follow the Prophets' guidance. That means discharging our duties and not adding to the faith of Islam anything that is not part of it.

Conversion to Islam is done by a very simple ritual. It is the duty of every Muslim to attract others to our faith.

Many people would like to have a copy of the Qur'an near to where they sleep. That is appropriate, provided that they do not have it for protection or blessing.

Iitihaf is staying in the mosque in order to devote oneself to worshiping for a certain period of time. No matter at what time of the year he stays in the mosque he may not have sex or sex play with his wife. If a women begins her menstruation while staying in the mosque she should leave straight away.

The wearing of wigs is *haraam* - not permissible.

Whenever you wish to read the Quran or to glorify Allah, you are strongly recommended to have ablution.

The view of the majority of scholars is that a woman in her menstruation and a man in the state of ceremonial impurity may not stay long in a mosque. They may pass through it but they cannot sit there for sometime.

Touching the feet of parents or other elder persons, seeking their blessing, is akin to acts of worship. Therefore, it is forbidden.

Prophet Ibrahim had to face a test - whether he would sacrifice his beloved son for the pleasure of Allah. Allah was pleased. He accepted the sacrifice. Just when the father blindfolded his son and was about to use the knife on him, God saved his life. The God-sent angel whisked away the child and in his place put a ram. It is this sacrifice which is commemorated by Muslims every year on Eid al-Adha.

If you take a bath in the type of bathroom which is common in our modern houses, when you cannot be seen by anyone, then it is perfectly all right to be totally undressed. You may supplement your shower with having ablution before you finish. If one is taking a shower for cleanliness, it does not include ablution. One has to add the ablution by going through its essentials, such as having the proper intention and washing one's face, hands and legs as well as wiping over a part of one's head. He should also add at least a few of what is recommended in ablution.

How do Muslims in Norway apply the timetable for prayer and fasting? What we need to realize is that Islam is practical religion. Hence such situations which are accidents of natural phenomena do not stop its teachings. We have a Hadith which tells us that in a day which is too long, we have to apportion time properly so as to conform in our prayers to the recognized standard of having five obligatory prayers in every 24 hours.

Maintaining good relations with Christian friends and relatives is recommended by Islam. As long as they do not adopt a hostile attitude to our faith or abuse the Prophet or speak ill of his companions. Such good relations, however, do not require or necessitate participation in their religious activities.

It is a Sunnah, or recommended practice, to call the athan close to the ears of a newborn baby. There are also two Hadiths which recommend calling the athan close to the right ear of a baby and iqamah (i.e. a shorter form of the athan made just before starting prayer) in his left ear.

The Prophet (peace be on him) passed by two graves and said, "They are suffering torment, yet they are not being punished for a major sin." He then said, "Yes, indeed. One of them was given to back biting, and one did not take precautions to avoid his urine splash". He then took a green plant and broke it into two and planted each part on one of the two graves. He then said, "It may be that their torment will be reduced as long as the two plants have not dried up."

Shweppes and Pepsi-Cola both say they use alcohol in processing their drinks. Hence it is right to ask whether they remain permissible or not. It is important to remind ourselves that what Allah has forbidden is what intoxicates, not a particular substance. No Qur'anic verse or Hadith refers to alcohol as forbidden. Any drink that intoxicates is forbidden. When intoxication is produced only by a very large amount of a particular drink then it is forbidden even to have a sip of it. Human experience shows that no one begins to have any intoxicating effect after drinking any amount of CocaCola or Pepsi-Cola. What is clear, therefore, is that the alcohol dissolves during the chemical interaction which results in the production of a new substance. We have, then, to apply the Islamic rule which states that a change of substance may lead to changing its position with regard to permissibility or otherwise.

Celebrating one's own or one's children's birthdays is a custom which some communities have borrowed from the Europeans. Therefore, if one marks such an occasion in imitation of non-Muslims, he is certainly at fault.

Islam has declared cursing and abusing, exchange of vulgar and obscene words an act of haraam (forbidden). There is only one cause of this sinning, and that is man is overcome by anger and he washes his hands of all decency and good manners. This is when the animal instinct becomes visible.

Q. Is it true that no type of bird flies over the Kaaba? If so, what is the reason.

A. I am not aware of anything that suggests that birds are prevented by divine power from flying over the Kaaba.

Q: Some people argue that a dog is no worse than a cat. Why is it then, that cats are allowed as pets, but dogs are not?

A: There is a basic difference between a cat and a dog. The dog is impure while the cat is not. Hence, it is not permissible to keep a dog in one's home as a pet. It is only permissible to have a dog for hunting and for tending sheep with a shepherd. No such restrictions apply to cats which are not impure.

BURIAL

Immediately after a person is dead it is better to clean him/her with a clean cloth. Prepare the following: Some kind of stand for washing the body; a few buckets of lukewarm water, a big mug, big bath or tub to let the used water flow into it. Hessian bags or old newspapers to absorb water spilled on the floor, soap, towel, sheet to cover the body and *Kafan* (shroud) in which the *May-yet* (corpse) is to be wrapped.

Keep the body covered with a sheet. Keep the private parts covered and avoid looking directly at it.

The Islamic mode of burial is another proof of brotherhood and equality. Whether you are rich or poor, there are no differently priced coffins according to class, but all must be buried in ordinary cloth.

Once the *May-yet* has been laid to rest, it is perfectly on order to make a prayer to Allah for forgiveness for the departed soul. One should, however, avoid doing anything at the graveyard, or elsewhere for that matter, which is not in conformity with Islamic teachings.

In the grave two angels come to the deceased and ask him about his faith and his view of Prophet Mohammed. A believer has his grave made as a wide expanse for him and his position in heaven is shown to him. A non-believer has his grave narrowed over him as if his ribs are going to crack. It is perfectly easy for Allah to have this done to a person who is cremated or drowned or eaten by whales or wild beasts.

Each sex washes his or her kind. If necessity arises, it is permissible for a husband or wife to wash each other.

"When a human being dies, all his actions come to an end, except in one of three ways: continuing act of charity, a useful contribution to knowledge or a God fearing, dutiful child who prays for him."

Concerning the position of burial of a dead person, it is recommended that the dead person is made to face the Qiblah in his burial place. If that is not easy, then any direction is all right.

If a person receives wages for merely reciting the Qur'an, as is done by some people who are hired to recite the Qur'an at the grave of a deceased person, or to recite it and request to grant its reward to the deceased, then earning money from this is forbidden.

Some scholars do maintain that women are not allowed to visit graves. In support of their view, they cite the Hadath which prevents women from following funerals and the one which quotes the Prophet as saying: "Allah curses the women who visit graves frequently and the ones who pray at them and put lanterns at them." A large number of scholars, however, are of the view that visiting graves is permitted for women. In support of their view they cite the Hadath of Lady Aisha, which is related by Al-Hakim on the authority of Abdullah ibn Mulaikah, who saw her coming back from visiting the grave of her brother, Abdurrahman. He asked her: "Had the Prophet prohibited this?" She said: "Yes, he had prohibited it, but he later encouraged visiting them (graves)."

It must be pointed out here that ignorant Muslims have introduced many un-Islamic customs into our society. Some throw flowers on the grave. This is extravagance and waste as they rot into filth and pollute the Magbarah (graveyard). Stones may be put around and over the grave to prevent the earth from spreading until it sets, or as a protection against it being dug up by animals. But solid constructions are un-Islamic.

A postmortem is permissible if it is conducted for the right purpose. We can say that determining the cause of death, either when a crime is suspected or to enable medical students and their teachers to learn about the effects of a certain diseases, is a legitimate purpose to carry out postmortem. Many people are under the impression that postmortems are forbidden in Islam.

Martyrs are given a special place in Islam. They are forgiven all their sins and they are admitted into heaven without having to face any reckoning to qualify for such a grade, a person actually sacrifices his life for Islam. It is certainly not right to equate a person who dies by drowning or accident or fire in the same with a person who is actively involved in Jihad and gets killed by the enemies of the Islam.

When you go to a grave of a pious or religious person in order to address your supplication there, your are assuming that your supplication is more likely to be answered there. This is certainly forbidden.

MEN AND WOMEN

The principle of equality of all human beings has always been central to the Islamic social concept. Equality also was established between man and woman. It was the normal practice throughout the world that women were considered far inferior to men. Islam addressed its message to both men and women and made it clear that both have the same rights and duties, with minor differences that are necessitated by their different natures and different roles in society .

Equal rights applies to a fetus once pregnancy is established. Anyone who causes abortion exposes himself to punishment.

A Muslim woman may not travel a distance which is covered in one whole day without being accompanied by her husband or a close relative whom she may not marry.

The Holy Quran gave women economic and social rights long before such rights were realized by Western women. In 1960, the government of the Kingdom of Saudi Arabia undertook the introduction of a national education program for girls. By the mid-1970s, about half of Saudi Arabian girls were attending school. Five years later, education was available to all Saudi girls. By 1980, there were six universities for women.

The Prophet has made it clear that when a woman travels she must have a man companion who is her husband or a *mahram*. This condition applies to all travel.

Horse riding is an activity encouraged by the Prophet. When a woman rides a horse, she must continue to observe Islamic standards of propriety. She may not wear clothes which are not acceptable from the Islamic point of view. The same applies with swimming.

When 47 women drove through the city last November to protest an unwritten ban on female driving, the *Matawa* listed the women's names and phone numbers in pamphlets branding them prostitutes and communists. The women lost their jobs, and the religious establishment issued a decree making the ban on driving official.

The Prophet tells us that when a man is alone with a woman, Satan is their third. This means that by being alone together, the man and the woman will start to have thoughts about things that are illegal. There is the temptation to do what is forbidden.

Islam forbids that a man stays with a woman alone

where they can have undisturbed privacy.

In Islamic society there were many a lady scholar. They all recognized the Wisdom of Islamic legislation and abided by its provisions. That helped them lead a happy life.

Concerning menstruation: I had a very strong prolonged flow of blood. I went to the Prophet to ask him about it. When I asked him if I had to stop praying and fasting, he said "Tie a cloth, and it will stop." I said, "It is greater than that." He said, "Curb it." I said, "It flows greatly." He then said, "You may do one of two things: either one will suffice. Which one you are able to do you know best. This is a strike from Satan. Be on your period for six or seven days, which Allah knows, and then perform *ghusl* until you see that you are clean. Pray for fourteen nights or thirteen nights and days and fast, and that will be sufficient for you. Do that every month as the other women become pure and menstruate. If you can, you may *ghusl* and pray the noon and afternoon prayers together. Delay the sunset and hasten the night prayers and pray them together. Perform *ghusl* for the morning prayer and pray it. This is how you may pray and fast if you have the ability to do so."

If it is menstruation blood, it is dark and recognizable. If you have that, abstain from prayer. If it is other than that, make ablution and pray.

The modern mosque invariably have separate facilities for ladies. These must include separate ablution and toilet areas. Where a mosque lacks separate accommodations for the women folk, they may form separate rows at the back of the men's row.

"Acquisition of knowledge is compulsory upon every Muslim, male AND FEMALE."

If a woman needs to have an internal examination and she has the option to go either to a lady doctor or a male doctor who are equally skilled and similarly specialized, then she must go to the lady doctor.

One of the problems facing the materialist society today is the indecision about women's role in the family and society. The proper remedy lies not in the prevailing individualism which causes women to forsake their responsibilities to husbands, parents and even children in their quest to be "liberated." This perceived freedom is creating a new kind of bondage for many women.

In the West the notion exists that there is very little if any difference between the two sexes in physical, intellectual and emotional endowment, and consequently there should be no difference in their role and functions in society. Hence the unisex society developed. The resulting effect of this idea of equality and equivalence has been to actually push women into imitating men and to despise their womanhood and femininity.

The unisex ideology creates competition between the sexes which is disastrous for society besides being unnatural.

The dual sex society, in contrast, has a natural attitude to sexual relationship and encourages cooperation rather than conflict between the sexes. Complementary to the unisex ideology is the sexist attitude of the chauvinistic materialists. We need not look beyond any Western magazine to see that the female and her sensuality is being abused do sell anything from motor cars and nuts and bolts to furniture and food.

Only in very recent times did the idea of sexual nondefinition achieve prominence, primarily in the Western societies. Even medical evidence pointing to emotional and mental difference between men and women are suppressed as it threatens the current trend of thought.

The Islamic attitude toward women is spelled out in the Quran. We make no excuse for veiling our women, we make no excuse for what is often perceived as "old fashioned" ideas. The truth is that Islam is never old-fashioned. The laws of Allah remain applicable whatever the century we live in or whatever the country - Muslim or non-Muslim - we happen to be in. Muslims have respect for all women, for the command from the Almighty is to "reverence the wombs (plural) that bore you".

About twenty ladies gathered at the International Islamic Relief Agency (Ladies Section) yesterday in Jeddah to attend a lecture on the importance of "Istigfar." A Muslim should always ask for forgiveness of Allah especially at times of agony. "We have to pray, recite the Quran and contemplate the holy verses so that we live in peace and prosperity. We have to endure troubles and keep patience at times of distress." Some ladies complained that their husbands beat them. One of the ladies replied that every family should tell their young men on the day of their wedding that they should behave kindly towards his wife.

It is the husband who is supposed to provide for the family. If he cannot gain enough to support the family, or if his income is too low to provide for a relatively acceptable standard of living, and provided the wife is willing, both of them may work for gain. However: 1. The husband has the right to terminate the wifes working whenever he deems it necessary; 2. He has the right to object to any job if he feels that it would expose his wife to any harm, seduction or humiliation; 3. The wife has the right to discontinue working whenever she pleases.

The veil is not part of Islamic terminology. Therefore, it has no Islamic definition. Linguistically speaking, the veil is something that a woman wears to cover her head and face. A Muslim woman is certainly required to dress modestly when she appears in public. She should wear loose clothes that cover all her body, with the exception of her face and the lowest part of her hands i.e., her palms.

Tinting a woman's hair is permissible provided that it

is not done in imitation of non-Muslim women. It is completely forbidden if a girl tints her hair solely because she saw some European women doing so, liked it and tried to imitate them. Regarding wigs for men, this is totally forbidden.

As a point of departure let me assure you that Islam treats women not necessarily as equal but as equivalent. In other words, whatever worth the woman has and whatever role she has to play in society, Islam sanctions that.

What you probably do not realize is that polygamy would lead to a flagrant violation of the sanctity of the woman's status in society. She could, for example, be accused of frivolous behavior without her being able to prove the contrary.

Polyandry - which means one woman having union with more than one man - is evidently an unnatural and devastating affair. It is biologically possible for a man to consort with a dozen women and yet be identified as the father of a dozen children. But it is impossible to identify the father of a single child whose mother had slept with more than one man.

In such situations the child is shunned as an illegitimate, because there is no definite proof as to who the father is. Imagine the chaos! The child is not any particular father's responsibility. Neither mother nor society will know whom to hold responsible. And the child grows up

without a sense of belonging, an outcast, mentally insecure.
This is playing havoc with human life! Polyandry, therefore,
is not biologically correct an is an unnatural act.

I have explained in the past that the veil is not obligatory
in Islam. A Muslim woman is not required to have a veil, but
she must cover all her body from head to toe with the exception
of her face and lowest part of her hands. This is different from
wearing a veil.

Scholars Study Women's Position In Islam: Women's
social economic and general conditions as well as cultural and
educational development in the Muslim world were the themes
of a seminar that concluded in Cairo. The three day seminar
was organized by the International Islamic Education Science
and Culture Organization, an OIC agency. Thirty seven scholars representing the agencies member countries took part in
the deliberations. The scholars and experts highlighted the
distinctive function of Muslim women within the family and
the society at large. Participants shed light on the rights and
duties of Muslim women in the context of the Islamic Shariah
which guarantees women's rights and protects their dignity as
human beings.

It is unfortunate that there have been misunderstandings regarding a womans position in Islam. This
misunderstanding is not only evident among non-
Muslims but also among certain individuals who are followers
of the religion with little or no knowledge of it. These people
set themselves as judges on what a woman should or should

not do. We have even witnessed in certain places the for-bidding of women from praying in the mosque. This is why we feel it is very important to clarify the views on this matter in Islam. Prayers in the Prophet's days were performed by Muslim women in their own section of the masjid behind the men. For the sake of solemnity and the seriousness of the occasion, they prayed in separate groups; however, both groups prayed in the masjid. Contrary to Western practice of a woman changing her "family name" by assuming that of her husband's giving an impression of her being a "property" to her husband, a Muslim woman retains her lineral name after marriage. Ibn Umar reported that the Messenger of Allah said: "Do not prevent the maid-servants of Allah from going to the mosque".

The pardah is the name of a special dress which prevails in certain Muslim countries. It fulfills the requirements of Islamic dress. What ever Muslim woman should do is not to appear before any man who is neither her husband nor a relative to whom she may not be married unless she wears something that meets the requirements of Islam. Her dress must be modest, somewhat loose so as not to describe the shape of her body. It is also important that her dress must not be transparent or eye-catching. It should not be an imitation of the dress of non-believing women.

It is important to understand that there is a part of the body of every human being which must be covered so that it may not be seen by others. That part of the body of a man extends, according to most scholars, from his waist line down to his knees. Some scholars are of the view that this part, which we call in Islamic terminology "Awrah" is limited to a man's private parts. All scholars agree that the Awrah of a woman includes all her body with the exception of her face and the lower parts of her arms, from the wrists downward. If a woman wants to read the Qur'an and she is alone or with other women, it is not obligatory for her to cover her head.

The concept of the sanctity of chastity and the protection of women can be found nowhere else except in Islam. The armies of the Western powers need the daughters of their own nations to satisfy their carnal appetites even in their own countries, and if they happen to occupy another country, the fate of its womenfolk can better be imagined than described.

Over a period of five years, the library of Sahara Islamic Cultural Centre was visited by a total of 420 readers. Some 125 of these were female, most of whom were Saudis, 43 were Saudi males most of whom were of an age which could no longer be considered young, and 352 were of other Arab nationalities. The Saudi women who are encumbered by household management and social circumstances were able to find time for reading whereas the listless Saudi young men who always complain of too much leisure could not find their way to knowledge which is a perplexing phenomenon we know not how to remedy, and a mistake for whom we know not to blame.

Muhammad Omar Al-Amoudy
29 August 1991

The objective of girls' education is to bring the girl up in a sound Islamic way so that she can fulfil her role in life as a successful housewife, ideal wife and good mother, and to prepare her for other activities that suit her nature such as teaching, nursing and medicine. Girls' education is conducted in an atmosphere of dignity, chastity and decency complying in all its forms and types with the provisions of Islam.

Article 155 of the educational policy in the Kingdom states that co-education is not allowed for boys and girls in all stages of education except in kindergartens and nurseries. Girls' education, in separate institutes, is mainly an issue related to the respected social status given to the woman by Islam as a wife and as a mother who builds up youth.

"Permissible love is permissible and forbidden one is forbidden". If the relationship between a married Muslim woman and a non-Muslim man is a fleeting relationship, then it is forbidden. On the other hand, if it is a serious exchange, which has a legitimate purpose, then it is permissible.

There is nothing wrong with the wish of ladies to be fashionable. What becomes problematic is the question: how to be so without infringing the laws of Shariah. To be fashionable does not mean to be promiscuous, does not mean to be less attractive to your husband. On the contrary, it is possible, and indeed desirable, for ladies to take pride in their appearance. But the precondition is that in doing so, they must ensure adherence in terms of Islamic criteria.

A lady can be thoroughly modern yet Islamically modest. In this way your own ego, your husband's rights and Islam's requirements are met.

It is true that the Prophet never shook hands with any women who was not his wife or a close relative. One is highly encouraged to avoid shaking hands with members of the opposite sex.

MARRIAGE

It is one of the main purposes of marriage that both husband and wife help each other maintain their chastity.

There is nothing wrong with taking contraceptive pills as long as they are safe for the woman taking them.

The dower is one of the conditions of a valid marriage contract. It is money payable by the husband to his wife and it becomes her own property and she has sole discretion with it the way she likes.

A man is not responsible to pay for the travel expenses of his wife in order that she fulfills the duty of pilgrimage.

It is forbidden for a Muslim to marry an adulterer or an adulteress. If a Muslim wants to marry a non-Muslim, she must become a Muslim first by conviction, not because it is convenient in the circumstances.

A Muslim woman may not marry any man who is not

a Muslim.

According to Islam, a Muslim may not marry any woman who is not a follower of Islam, Christianity, or Judaism.

When two people get married it is the man who is responsible to manage the affairs of his family. He is the bread winner and he must support his wife and children, providing them with a decent home depending on his income and circumstances. He must feed his wife and children, clothe them and ensure their proper housing.

Shaving the hair of the newborn is also commended in order to weigh up the hair and give to charity the value of its weight in gold or silver. By shaving the hair you give the infant a good chance to strengthen the roots of the hair.

Muslims may attend wedding ceremonies as long as the ceremony does not contain some pagan ritual.

When first cousins get married, as it is allowed in Islam, they should make sure that their children do not marry within the same family.

It is forbidden for a man to hit his wife on her face. That is the worst humiliation. Besides, we have some very important organs in our heads.

While Islam has given a husband the right to discipline a disobedient wife, it has left only a very small room for hitting her as a last resort when all efforts to make her see reason have failed.

It is also not permissible for a Muslim to hurl verbal abuse on his wife. It is needless to say that verbal abuse creates ill feelings.

The Prophet portrays beating a women in a very bad light, as he says: "How is it that only one of you could beat his wife as he beats a slave. When he may have intercourse with her at the end of the day?"

It is not permissible for a women who believes in Allah to admit into her husband's home anyone whom he does not like to be admitted, or to go out when he disapproves, or to obey anyone against her husband, or to banish herself from his bed, or to hit him (if she is stronger than him).

A women is required to obey her husband but he also must consider her wishes and preferences. We are simply speaking about an ultimate possibility to which recourse can be made when differences cannot be amicably resolved.

If a quarrel takes place between a man and his wife and he wants to send her to her parents home, she may go.

A man does not need his first wife's permission in order to marry another woman. Allah has granted him this privilege. The main requirement is to treat his two wives fairly.

A marriage contract is an agreement between a man and a woman to get married. It's consistent elements: A commitment and acceptance. The commitment is made by the woman's guardian to marry the woman in his charge to the man against the payment of a specified dower. The man declares his acceptance of the commitment.

From an Islamic point of view, a man is allowed to have four wives. If he wants to marry a second wife he does not need to have any justification other than doing what is permissible.

If a woman is pregnant at the time a marriage contract is made the marriage is not valid. It is not permissible for a Muslim to marry a pregnant woman until she has given birth. "Anyone who believes in Allah and the last day must not irrigate with his water a seed planted by another person."

It often happens that when a man dies leaving behind a young widow and young children that it is found appropriate that the brother of the deceased marry his brother's widow and look after his children. The woman has to observe the normal waiting period of four months and ten days from the day of her husband's death. If she is pregnant at the time of his death, her waiting period extends until she has given birth. The new marriage cannot take place during the waiting period. A waiting period applies only to women.

What is not permissible from the Islamic point of view is to be married to two sisters at the same time. When marriage to one sister is over, either through divorce or death, the man may marry her sister.

Both man and wife must help each other maintain their chastity. If there is a boycott between the two, then such boycott creates the temptation to go outside the bond of marriage in order to fulfill a natural urge.

Many scholars maintain that in the presence of a woman's father, no one else may act for her in her marriage.

It is permissible for a man to marry more than one woman, the same is not permissible to a woman. She cannot have more than one husband at the same time. You must not start thinking about another man until you are free to marry that man. While you are married to your husband, every thought of marrying another one is wrong and every action is forbidden.

In Islam, the Prophet makes it clear that the choice of a marriage partner should be made on the basis of each party's strength of faith.

Choosing a wife is an important matter in a man's life because it has a great effect on building the family and the society as well.

Emphasizing the importance of his choice, Prophet Mohammed (Peace Be Upon Him) said: "A women is married for having four distinguishing features: her wealth, noble descent, beauty and being religious, so choose the religious one and you will win."

One of the proverbs says: "Get married from (the family of) people who have the same habits as yours." In other words, the boys and girls whom the wife give birth to, inherit the manners and habits of their mother's relatives. So when one gets married from a good and noble family with a good social background, the children will have good manners and habits and vice versa.

A wife of no noble descent is not likely to be good and honest and so will her children be.

Getting married from people who do not have the same religious belief is not encouraged, since it has a bad effect on the husband, the children and consequently the society. "He who gets married from people who have a different religion will die of illness."

On choosing a good husband, the Prophet (pbuh) says: "If someone is religious and honest comes to you proposing for marriage, do not deny him."

One old and common attitude that is still adopted by some people is that the husband should be firm with his wife, especially in the early period of their marriage so that he will be awesome and his word will carry more weight.

As they say, "A horse is known by its rider and a woman by her husband."

It is permissible for a Muslim man to marry a Christian woman, without converting her to Islam. Indeed, he should give her appropriate facilities to practice her faith, without pressuring her to convert to Islam. She may live with him as a Christian for the rest of her life. He should certainly explain to her the Islamic faith and tell her that Allah requires her and everyone else to be a Muslim. The choice should remain hers only. Their children in this case are Muslim, because he is a Muslim. The rule which is applied to all inter-faith marriages is that in matter of religion the children follow the parent who belongs to the higher faith. Islam is certainly the highest, then comes Christianity and then Judaism.

When a women embraces Islam, she should notify her husband of the fact. He has the choice either to follow her suit and become a Muslim or to continue to follow his religion. The time such a husband is given to declare whether he wants to be a Muslim or not is equal to a womans waiting period which she has to observe if her husband dies or if she is divorced. If such a period lapses and her husband does not become a Muslim, their marriage is deemed to have been dissolved. She now observes a waiting period and when this period lapses, she is free to get married to a Muslim man.

Scholars agree that if a mans work necessitates that he should be absent from home, he can do that for a maximum period of four months without the need to have his wife's agreement to his absence. If he must stay longer, then that absence must be by mutual consent.

Where both spouses are above the age of puberty, it is the duty of the husband, and not that of the wife as happens in some Western countries nowadays, to supply his wife and children with food, clothes and lodging on a scale commensurate with the social position of the partners and in accordance with the customs and habits of the society in which they live.

If the wife is a minor, she will be maintained by her father or guardian as we have seen before. The Messenger of Allah married A'isha two years before she reached the age of puberty and did not give her maintenance.

It is not essential to provide one's wife with maintenance in the following events:
1. If she packed and moved out of her matrimonial

home to some other place without her husband's permission or without religious cause.

2. If she traveled without his permission.

3. If she puts on Ihram for haj without his permission.

4. If she refused sexual intercourse to her husband.

5. If she is imprisoned after committing a crime.

6. If the husband dies and she becomes a widow.

A wife is entitled to demand her husband, about to set out on a journey, either to give her, for the whole duration of his absence, an anticipatory allowance, or to give a power of attorney to another for her maintenance.

Q. What I would like to know is whether I am married to my man, although we have not signed any marriage contract. Our "marriage" took place in an office when I was in one room and everyone else was in another because they were all men. We had witnesses who, as they came out at the end of the "ceremony"' offered congratulations to me. Since I did not have any relatives to celebrate the marriage, we simply went out together, just the two of us. Because I feel I am not properly wed, I have asked him on two separate occasions whether we are married and he answered in the affirmative. Yet no one in his family knows about our marriage. I live with them in the same house but separate flats. As I have become a Muslim with full conviction, I want to be sure.

Uncertain lady

A. What you should do now is to insist that your marriage is properly registered with the civil authorities. Your husband cannot deny you that because you are only asking to document a legal relationship. Perhaps the best way is to arrange for the marriage to be properly made at an Islamic court. Once this is done, your position is clear. But you should stop any marital relationship with him unless you are sure that the marriage that took place is a proper and valid one. This means that you have given power of attorney to someone to act for you and he acted according to the mandate you have given. If not, you must do it now. You must not lose any time.

The Qur'anic verse which states that an adulterer may marry only an adulteress does not mean that such a person is doomed and whoever he will marry will turn out to have committed adultery in the past. That is a totally different sense which is not meant by the Qur'anic statement. The Qur'anic rule means that it is not permissible that a man who is known to commit adultery to marry a chaste Muslim woman. Indeed, if he proposes to marry such a woman, he must be turned back. The same applies in the reverse case. An adulteress may not be married to a chaste Muslim man. Indeed, it is forbidden for him to propose to her or marry her. If either adulterer repents of what he or she had done and resolves not to repeat it, he or she is treated as someone who has not committed a sin. When we are sure that repentance is genuine, we may help them marry in the same way as we help any Muslim to get married.

It is not permissible for a Muslim to adopt a child who is not created from his own sperm because this is against the Islamic teachings.

The practices which are recommended for a newly born child are well known: Calling the athan close to his ears shortly after he is born, choosing a good name for him, shaving his hair weighing it and donating to charity the equivalent of the weight of the hair in gold and silver, and the aqeeqah which is the slaughter of a sheep or two on the 7th, 14th or 21st day of his birth and inviting neighbors and relatives to a dinner when the meat of the slaughtered sheep is served.

The word "justice" means the equal treatment of all the wives in providing them with material means and necessities of life such as those of the pocket money, clothes, accommodation and the like, so that all wives enjoy the same degree of satisfaction from the privileges. However, it is rather difficult for any human being to control his feelings towards his wives and to consequently be just to them. Such justice is something unrealistic and impossible too. But what is more important for the husband is that he should be fair in showing his feelings to his wives.

The other point which I would like to emphasize is that there is no virtue in polygamy from the Islamic point of view. When a person marries more than one wife, he is likely to have a large family, and if he is unable to provide for his family, then he is actually imposing a life of poverty on big number of people. This is absolutely unnecessary.

When the dower system is reversed so as to make the bridegroom the beneficiary, the bride is deprived of something which Allah has assigned to her by right. The problem is bypassed in most cases with a nominal agreement between the two families that the bridegroom will pay a specified amount to his wife. On the night of the wedding, the bride is instructed by her family to tell her husband that she forgoes the amount of the dower agreed between them. This is certainly a travesty of the Islamic system.

People normally prefer to marry women who are younger than them for practical purposes. A young wife is always more appealing to her husband than an elderly one. Moreover, she is better able to look after her husband and her children. There is no restriction on ages of husband and wife. A man may marry a woman who is much younger or much older than him. The same applies in the reverse order.

Every woman who was breast-fed by your mother either before or after you, is your sister by suckling, if the suckling was for five times or more. Therefore, the girl who was breast-fed by your mother together with your sister is a sister to you. As such, you cannot marry her. The same is the case with all your other brothers — elder and younger — who, too, cannot enter wedlock with that girl. You and all your brothers have to treat her just like a sister.

There is a general rule which applies to other cases of suspected parenthood. It states that "The child belongs to the man on whose bed it is born, while the adulterer bites the dust." On the basis of this rule, if a married woman is a victim of rape and she gets pregnant, her husband is the father of her child. If she is not married, she brings the child up and the rapist again "bites the dust".

There are no practices restricted for married people, that are permissible for unmarried ones. The society Islam establishes is characterized by its serious attitude to morality. It does not allow young people to indulge in excesses, then requires them to stop these when they get married. That may be characteristic of other societies, but not an Islamic one. Islam encourages early marriages, in recognition of the natural tendencies of young people. The Islamic philosophy is such that it does not consider a natural tendency as wrong or evil. It provides a legitimate framework for its fulfillment. Thus, sexual urge is a natural one. Marriage is the accepted institution for its fulfillment and the safeguarding of the rights of all parties concerned with such fulfillment.

Scholars have made a rule which covers all marriages between relatives. They say that it is not permissible for a man to be married to two women who are related to each other, if their relation is such that it would have blocked their own marriage, had one of them been a man. This means that it is permissible to be married to a woman and her cousin at the same time.

The fact of the birth of your child seven months and one week after your wedding does not allow you to entertain any doubt about your wife's moral behavior. It is perfectly possible for a woman to give birth after that period. Doctors make it clear that it is possible to give birth after twenty-six weeks of conception. This is in line with the view of old Muslim scholars who suggest that the minimum period of pregnancy is six months, after which a live birth is possible. It is also possible for a woman to conceive on the first occasion when her marriage is consummated. Such a birth is possible from the medical and religious points of view.

Twenty-eight couples got married in a group marriage function organized by the town of Al-Qara. This was organized to reduce marriage expenses. The maximum and minimum amounts of dowries in this mass marriages were SR25,000 and SR5,000 respectively. Similar functions were organized in the city nine years ago when 40 young men and women were married in one night there.

All wedding houses and hotels where wedding parties are held are obliged to end such parties at 12 o'clock midnight and to prohibit extension of time. A circular was sent to the directors of Virtues and Prevention of Vice Organizations, and the Western region police. The circular commented on lengthy parties held in marriage houses and the distress and problems they caused women and their guardians. Men should not be permitted to enter women's halls, and that all wedding houses and hotels should be informed on the necessity to comply with the order. Those who violate the order will be subject to deterrent penalties.

High dower are still a problem despite the agreements among tribes at reducing them. Many husbands are still suffering from the burden of debts taken previously to pay the high dower and other demands from the bride's fathers. There are many other young men who are hesitant to marry due to this high dower and other conditions put by the girl's fathers. The leaders of this country have given this problem a lot of attention by urging fathers to facilitate matters concerning marriage since this will be great benefit to the individual and society. According to the Sharia there is nothing that prevents a man from specifying a certain dower for his daughter. Exorbitant dower is a big defect in society necessitating intervention to mend it because its harm does not affect the bride and bridegroom only but it extends to the society as a whole.

Adoption means to give somebody your name though he does not belong to you for he is created from sperms belonging to another person. Therefore adoption is considered as one of the greatest sins. It is not permissible for a Muslim to adopt a child who is not created from his own sperm because this is against the Islamic teachings.

According to the Islamic Shariah, a Muslim is the one who accepts the two Shahadahs (articles of faith) and declared his conversion to Islam. And thus, he will be treated as a Muslim in all the affairs of life. Within this concept, if he is found that he does not practice the obligatory rites out of recklessness he will be considered a disobedient Muslim. In such a case, you must advise and urge him to repent of this wrong behavior. And if it was proved that he was doing this intentionally, then you must stop sexual relationship with him and end your marriage as well.

Islam says that a good Muslim wife obeys her husband and also says that a good Muslim husband takes care of his wife. You have explained at length your wife's habits and I agree that, if the situation is as you describe, it creates a very unhealthy family atmosphere. If the problems persists, the options open to you are detailed in the Qur'an. There is a gradual method of trying to bring discipline into a family when the wife is totally indisciplined. It is not permissible to move to the next stage until the previous one has been tried in a reasonable manner and for a reasonable period of time. This stage is to give sound advice and to remind one's wife of her duties and that if she persists, she will have to account to Allah for her misbehavior. If such admonition fails, then the next stage is to use separate bedrooms for a while, indicating that this measure has been adopted because of her misbehavior. If this method also fails, then Allah has allowed a husband to beat his wife in order to discipline her, but has made it clear that this beating should not be very painful and that he must not hit her in the face. If none of these methods succeeds, then one should consider a divorce.

DIVORCE

If a wife dislikes to stay with her husband and she feels that she may not be fulfilling her obligations toward him as a wife, or that he may not fulfill his obligation toward her then she can request the nullification of her marriage through the court. She must be prepared to pay her husband compensation for termination of their marriage. The breakup of a marriage at the wife's request is different from divorce in that no maintenance is payable by the husband to his wife during the waiting period. Her waiting period lasts only until she has her first period of menstruation after the termination of her marriage.

It is forbidden to divorce a women when she is in her menstruation period, or if she is free from menstruation but they have had intercourse after her last menstruation.

To divorce a wife the husband declares that he divorces her, but pronounces the word of divorce once only. It is forbidden to say it three times in secession. She then starts her waiting period using a separate bedroom. When the waiting period is over the divorce is complete.

The husband has to support the wife during the waiting period and she need not cook for him or do any household duties.

If the divorce has taken place for a third time, they cannot remarry until she has married another man which should be a full and complete marriage, intended to last until either of them dies.

There is no disagreement among scholars that to divorce one's wife three times or more on the same occasion is forbidden from the Islamic point of view because it is an abuse of a legitimate procedure.

Scholars mention that divorce in anger does not take effect. But that means that the divorcing man should be in a state of blind anger which does not enable him to realize what he is actually saying. To judge whether this ruling applies to any particular case, the man should be asked after he has cooled down whether he realizes that he has divorced his wife. If he says no, then the divorce does not take effect. If he was aware of it, then the divorce is valid. The fact that he has mentioned the word of divorce three times on one occasion is immaterial. This is a single time divorce which is revocable.

The responsibility of maintenance of the husband is not only when the woman lives as a legal wife and towards his children by that wife, but it is important to maintain her even in the event of divorce. As for the child, its nursing, welfare and the home of the mother remains the duty of the father. If the mother's milk fails or if such circumstances arise which bar the natural course of the mother's nursing the child, merits the father's responsibility to give the child to someone else to suckle at his own expense. The mothers shall give suck to their off-spring for two whole years. If the father desires to complete the term, but he shall bear the cost of their food and clothing on equitable just terms.

When a man writes "I divorce you" three times on a piece of paper and sends it to his wife this divorce counts as one, although he has written it three times. The reinstatement of marriage is possible after the first and second divorce. But if divorce takes place three times, then the reinstatement cannot take place until the woman has married another man and lived with him in the normal way and at a later date he either dies or divorces her. If he wants to cancel his divorce and reinstate his marriage, then he has to approach his divorcee about that, and, if she agrees, he should marry her again. If she is still in her waiting period, this can be done by mutual agreement and bringing in two witnesses.

When someone says or writes to his wife that he has divorced her, she should receive what has been said or written very seriously and act on it. The fact that he was angry at the time does not affect of validity of the divorce, because he was aware of what he was doing. It is only when a man is in a state of blind anger at the time when he divorces his wife that the divorce is not valid. I mean "blind anger" literally. The man would be in a situation

where he does not known what he is doing . If he picks up
a piece of paper and writes down what he wants to write, he
cannot, then, be described as having been in a state of blind
rage.

SEX

Sex is a reality and, therefore, parents should discuss it with children. Because if they don't, there is likelihood that children would make a wrong decision and harm themselves morally and physically. But these matters should not be discussed in third or fourth grades, as is done in some Western schools. One does not need to know about fire arms until he or she is a certain age. The same applies to these intimate issues.

The contemporary society has stooped so low that it does not consider homosexuality and sodomy as crimes. In some countries in the West the "rights" of homosexuals are protected.

Contemporary "civilizations" which regard bygone days and its people as barbarous, savages and heathen, has stooped lower through its insistence that it is the right of mankind to freely choose to be homosexual if they so please.

Homosexuality, which has become acceptable as normal and indeed part of human rights, will never be accepted by Islam as normal or sanctioned as a human right. The transgressor will suffer in hell for a thousand years.

Islam has a very serious moral outlook. Hence, it requires its followers to confine the fulfillment of their sexual urge within the marriage. It is one of the main duties of a woman toward her husband that she should respond when he needs her. If she does not, she actually pushes him toward seeking satisfaction elsewhere.

When a wife refuses the advances of a husband, men may be pushed into unlawful practices. That helps spread immorality within the Muslim community. Therefore, Islam deals with this question at the source, making it one of the obligations of a wife to respond to her husband.

Most Muslim scholars agree that the shortest possible duration of pregnancy is six months, after which a woman may give birth to a developed baby. If a woman gives birth after six months, it is not possible for anyone to accuse her of adultery.

The full period for breast feeding extends to two years. The total period of pregnancy and breast-feeding is 30 months. Simple arithmetic shows that a pregnancy for six months is possible.

The woman's punishment for fornication is flogging with 100 lashes.

"We still have music. This makes people want to drink wine and sleep with women".

"If women don't cover up, they will have sex with everyone, like in the US."

There are no steps or measures which Islam imposes on a husband if a man discovers that his wife has been in contact with a man during his absence. He has to deal with the situation as he thinks fit, provided that he does not exceed the limits of Islamic decency. He should not keep a woman guilty of adultery as his wife.

It may be useful to remember here the ruling concerning a man who finds his wife committing adultery and cannot have witnesses. He has to swear five times that he has seen her committing the act of adultery and he should incur in the fifth oath Allah's curse on himself if his statement be not true. When he has done this, the woman is liable to be punished for adultery unless she makes a similar denial. She has to swear five times that she is innocent of the charge, combining the fifth oath with her incurring Allah's anger if her statement be untrue. If she does so, the two are automatically divorced and cannot be remarried in any circumstances.

Q. Is drinking water immediately after intercourse harmful to health?

A.N.S.S.

A. It is always advisable to avoid drinking water

immediately after intercourse as it is true after every exercise.

Dr. Ghozzi

Islam requires Muslim girls who have attained puberty to cover themselves when they appear in public, making sure that all their bodies are well covered with the exception of their faces and the lower parts of their hands, up to the wrists. As you see, this ruling does not relate the action required to a particular age. It relates it to a stage of development. I am afraid I cannot change the ruling. Nor can anyone on earth. This is a ruling of Islam.

Q. Scholars in my home country say that a Muslim in heaven will have 62 most beautiful women as a gift. Please comment.

A: Allah tells us in the Qur'an that among the aspects of grace He gives to the believers whom he admits into heaven is the company of pretty, large eyed female creatures. What we should understand is that those large eyed beautiful females in heaven are not substitutes for our wives on earth. They are part of the grace Allah bestows on His servants with whom he is pleased.

ABLUTION

It is infinitely better and more appropriate to have a fresh ablution when one has touched his private parts.

As for touching a person of the opposite sex (apart from one's mother, sister, daughter, or niece), the Shafie school of thought is of the view that any such physical contact invalidates ablution.

A deliberate contact when one is conscious that he is holding the hand of a woman or touching her requires a new ablution.

Tayammum - "aim, purpose." In Islamic law it refers to "aiming for or seeking" soil to wipe one's face and hands with the intention of preparing oneself to pray.

"And if you are ill, or on a journey or one of you comes from relieving himself, or you have touched women, and you do not find water, then go to high clean soil and rub your face and hands there with."

Tayammum is permissible only on specific occasions, these are:

(a) One cannot find water, or the amount one finds is insufficient for ablution.

(b) One is injured or ill. If one is in this condition, and believes water will worsen it, he does not have to be absolutely sure, but may base his opinion on past experience or what a knowledgeable person has told him.

(c) If water is cold enough to physically harm the user. This is only allowed on the condition that he can find no one to heat it, or is unable to use the public bathrooms.

(d) When water is nearby, but one does not want to fetch it due to fear. If one fears for his life, family, wealth for example, if an enemy is nearby, one may perform *Tayammum*. This is also allowed if there is water but one lacks the proper means to get it, or if one fears some accusation against him if he gets it.

(e) If one is saving his water for later use. This could be for making dough, cooking or to remove an impurity.

(f) If one can get water, but fears that prayer will be over by the time he gets it. He can perform *tayammum* and pray.

(g) The soil used for *tayammum* must be pure soil. This can be sandstone, gypsum and so on.

Sea water is not impure. The purity of sea water is based on the Prophet's words: "It's (the sea) water is pure and it's (dead) animals are lawful." The saltiness of the sea has nothing to do with the matter, it remains pure and permissible for ritual ablution.

When one wakes up a few minutes before sunrise, he

should proceed immediately to get ready for prayers. In the case of having a wet dream or being in the state of ceremonial impurity, he should proceed to remove it by taking a shower. If he must heat the water because it is too cold and he fears for himself, he should proceed to do that.

It is not necessary to perform ablution after eating camel meat. When the Prophet was having camel meat with his companions, one of them released wind. In order not to embarrass the person the Prophet said it was not necessary to do ablution after eating camel meat.

It is the view of most scholars that to touch one's private parts, skin to skin, invalidates ablution. If you touch your private parts, when you are drying yourself after having had grand ablution, you need to have ablution, i.e., Wudhu, before praying.

Most scholars are of the view that any person who is in a state of ceremonial impurity, which is the result of ejaculation or menstruation, or after intercourse, may not read the Qur'an until he or she has had the grand ablution, i.e., ghusl, whi involves washing all one's body.

Although smoking is forbidden in Islam, it does not invalidate ablution. Nor does watching ordinary television programs have any effect on the validity of your ablution.

It is sufficient to perform *ghusl* for both menstruation and sexual impurity, or for the Friday prayer and the '*id* prayer, or for sexual impurity and the Friday prayer, if one has the intention for both of them. If a person performed post-sex *ghusl* but did not make ablution the *ghusl* will suffice. It is acceptable for a person in post-sex uncleanliness or a menstruating woman to remove their hairs, cut their nails, go to the markets, and so on, without dislike. One may enter a public bathroom as long as he keeps his private parts from being seen, and he does not look at others' private parts.

No, it is not appropriate to start ablution with the name of Allah if one is doing it in the bathroom where there is a toilet. Mentioning the name of Allah in the bathroom is wrong. People obviously need to do the ablution in bathrooms and they have learned that many supplications are recommended when they wash different parts of their body as part of their ablution. It is true that every action of a Muslim is recommended to start with "bismillah", which means "in the name of Allah" But even then, one should not say this phrase in a bathroom where there is a toilet. It is sufficient if he is only conscious of that without giving his consciousness any vocal or verbal expression.

A woman need not undo her hair when she performs her grand ablution. What she should do is to take some water with her cupped hands and wet her hair with it rubbing it through. She does that three times before pouring water over the rest of her body and washing it properly. When she does that, her grand ablution is complete.

PRAYER

Is it permissible to offer prayers wearing clothes which may bear the picture of an animal? If a picture is printed on a dress, it may be used for prayer. However, if it is stitched on it and can be removed without damaging the garments, then it is better removed.

Prayers can be offered anywhere with the exception of particular spots such as graveyards, bathrooms, etc. The only thing you have to do is determine the right direction.

A person who has missed prayer for any period of time and for any reason need not compensate for it by offering additional prayers for a similar period. This means that when the time has passed, a missed prayer cannot be offered.

It is forbidden to pray after the morning prayers until the sunrise and from the sunrise until the sun has risen to the length of a spear above the horizon, and when the sun is at its meridian until it moves slightly to the west, and after the afternoon prayer until the sun sets.

Pray the morning prayers and then abstain from praying until sunrise and the sun has completely risen, for it rises between the horns of Satan. That is when the unbelievers prostrate to it. After the afternoon prayer, abstain from praying until the sun sets, for it sets between the horns of Satan, and that is when the unbelievers make prostrate to it.

There is no evidence whatsoever that it is preferred to cover one's head while praying.

Anyone who is unable to find the direction of the Qiblah because of it being cloudy, dark or generally being lost, must ask someone who does know to point him in the right direction. His prayers are correct and even if he subsequently discovers that the direction was indeed wrong, he need not repeat these prayers.

If the correct direction for prayer remains unknown for a long time, one should ascertain the direction before every prayer.

With the ending of the odd prayer, the evening prayer and the five prayers are complete. In this way the Muslim spends his day and night in worship, obedient, and sincerity, exaltation, thanks and prayer to God, just as he awoke in the morning.

Let me tell you first that Allah was fully aware of the

difficulty of a requirement to human beings to pray 50 times everyday. He has made it so in order to give the Muslim community the privilege of earning the reward of 50 prayers while doing five.

Whoever catches a *rakaah* of prayer before its time has expired has caught the entire prayer in its time.

There is no doubt it is forbidden to have a mosque within a graveyard or to pray facing a grave.

The Prophet is quoted in an authentic Hadith as saying: "When the *iqamah* is called, then no prayer may be offered than the obligatory one. "This means that once the call is made to start the congregational prayer, then no voluntary prayer of whatever description may be offered until the congregation have completed their obligatory prayer. This is due to the fact that Islam dislikes any action or gesture which suggests that the Muslim community is not totally united.

The bona fide traveller may commence performing prayers in the *Qasar* method immediately upon leaving his city or village boundaries. It is furthermore a rule that the journey needs to be approximately thirty one and a half miles long before *Qasar salaah* becomes permissible.

It is also a rule for the correctness of *Qasar* that the traveller should not at any time follow a non-traveller or a traveller performing his *salaah* in the itmaam (i.e in full) manner, while he performs his *salaah* in the *Qasar* manner.

It is reported that Umar ibn Al Khattah once led the dawn prayer. After he left, he discovered the trace of a wet dream on his clothes. When he discovered the trace he said: "I have indeed grown old. I have indeed grown old." He meant that in his old age, he could not remember having had a wet dream. He took a shower, repeated his prayer ordering no one to repeat theirs.

Each obligatory prayer has a time range during which it must be offered. Dawn, or *Fajr* prayer, for example, must be offered after the break of dawn, but before sunrise. This means that we have approximately one and a half hours when we must offer Fajr prayer. When the sun has risen, the time for this particular duty has lapsed and this prayer cannot be offered.

Prayer Schedule: September

Makkah	Jeddah	Madina	Riyadh	Tabuk
4:52	4:55	4:51	4:23	5:01
12:12	12:15	12:13	11:45	12:25
3:37	3:40	3:39	3:10	3:51
6:15	6:18	6:16	5:47	6:27
7:45	7:48	7:46	7:17	7:57

If the delay for prayer was caused by oversleeping, this is one of the reasons which allow a prayer to be offered after its time-range has lapsed. The other situation is to have forgotten that particular prayer completely.

When traveling the voluntary and traditional prayers may be shortened to two rakaahs only for the morning prayer and the odd prayer. Shortening the prayer is a dispensation and gift from God to the worshippers who fear Him and they must accept the gift. You are therefore required to shorten the prayer while traveling and this is an obligatory duty. There is no difference whether you are traveling by air, car, ship train, camel, or on foot.

If you join the Friday congregation before the prayer has started, you have joined it well in time and you add nothing to Friday prayer. Similarly, if you join the congregation after prayer has started but you manage to catch the first *rak 'ah* with the imam you add nothing to your prayer. If you arrive later than that, and you cannot catch up with him in the first *rak'ah*, then complete your prayer to four *rak' ahs* instead of two. You are in this case, offering *Dhuhr* instead of Friday prayer.

If you fall asleep in the Mosque while waiting for prayer call you will not have to perform a new ablution if you fall asleep while setting up. If you fall asleep laying down you will have to perform a new ablution. It is not possible to pass wind while setting.

Scholars are in agreement that joining a congregation at distant mosque making use of the radio in order to follow the movements of the imam is not correct. A congregation is one whole body and it cannot be separated by objects or areas lying in between its members and the imam. It must be a continuous congregation.

Concerning shoes, which is the main area of confusion, Abu Saeed reported that the Prophet removed his shoes. The congregation then also removed theirs. When he asked them why they removed their shoes, they replied they did so because he removed his. The Prophet said that the Angel Gabriel came and informed him that there was some dirt on his shoes. "Therefore when you come to the mosque you should turn your shoes around and examine them. If he finds some dirt on it he should rub it against the ground and pray in it".

The Asr prayer begins in the afternoon when the shadow of an object is of the same length as the object itself, and continues until the sun sets.

Why do matawwas tell people to pray? Allah has explained that this community is the best community for mankind. They are the most beneficial to them, supremely kind towards them, because they have perfected the enjoining on people of what is proper and forbidding them what is improper, since they have commanded every right and forbidden every wrong to everyone. This they have performed through struggle in God's cause with themselves and with their property, and this is the perfection of benefit for mankind. From the foregoing you will clearly learn that it is the duty of every Muslim - not only those members of the Board for Enjoining Virtue and Preventing Vice. We need to thank Allah for these people who regard our religion so important that they do not waiver one inch from performing their duty as Muslims, which after all is also your duty and mine.

Ladies are exempt from the requirement of attending congregational prayers in the mosque. This is due to the nature of their role in looking after young children and household duties.

The term called "qada'" signifies the attendance to a duty after its time has lapsed. When this is related to prayer, it actually refers to a person who has missed an obligatory prayer and wants to offer it after it has lapsed. Some scholars say that this is necessary and that if a person prays "qada", then the sin of missing an obligatory prayer is removed. The weightier opinion is that no compensation can be made for a prayer which is missed through negligence. There is an exception however, made by the Prophet in two cases: Sleeping through the time range of a prayer or loss of consciousness through illness or accident, etc., and forgetfulness.

Wearing socks when one prays is perfectly valid.

Large areas of the Muslim world today have adopted the Western style of dress, which includes a suit, a shirt and a tie. In these areas no one thinks of this type of menswear as an imitation of non-believers. Hence, it is permissible to wear it. Similarly, it is permissible to wear a tie in prayer.

It is forbidden to deliberately cross the path of a person while he is offering prayers. This applies whether the worshipper is offering his prayers at home or in a mosque or anywhere else. Scholars make it clear, therefore, that before starting prayer the worshiper should put some sort of screen just a little distance further than the spot where he puts his head on the ground when he prostrates himself. That screen could be any object a stick, a book, a shopping bag, his shoes, etc.

Is prayer valid if one wears a wig? Is it okay to wear a wig? Is transplant okay? This question involves three separate points. The first is the one which concerns the validity of ones prayers while wearing a wig. The answer to this point is that his prayers are valid. It is not right to attach the validity of prayers to something which has no bearing on it. The second point concerns the wearing of a wig. This is something that Islam does not approve, for men or women. If hair transplant is felt by specialists to be successful, then we apply to it the same ruling which concerns organ transplant. This is permissible as long as it is beneficial to the recipient, without adversely affecting the donor.

New regulations stipulating that federal government officials in Pakistan should stop work for 30 minutes of afternoon prayers have upset some Pakistanis. Before that, the interruption was interpreted as a tea or lunch break although the faithful also used the opportunity to say prayers. General Zia not only designated the break for prayers but also expected department heads to set a good example by leading the faithful Muslims who interpret Islam as a progressive, scientific and rational religion, devoid of empty rituals, point out that the longest interval between the five prayers ordained by Islam per day is eight to ten hours between the "Fajr" and "Zuhr" - the pre-dawn and midday prayers. "It is ordained to enable believers to put in eight hours or so of uninterrupted work to earn an honest living," wrote Gilani and requested the government to reconsider "this break business". - DPA.

PILGRIMAGE

Annually great hordes of Muslims converge from all directions and from all parts of the earth on the Sacred Mosques - the house of Allah - where they realize that they are a part of a great Islamic brotherhood which knows no human barriers based on race, nationality or colour.

Islam is a religion of ease and practically.

Pilgrimage is defined as a journey to the sacred mosques in Makkah which includes *tawaf*, *sa'ie*, attending Arafat and completing all the duties of a pilgrim. If he leaves offering his duty from one year to another, he may die before he has fulfilled his duty.

If a Muslim determines to go for pilgrimage, or Umrah he should do the following before he embarks on his journey

1. Urge his family, friends and relatives to observe the Islamic teachings and to abide by Allahs commandments.

2. Write down any loans he owes to others or he has given to others, so that everybody's right is documented.

3. Write his will.

4. Repent all his past sins and mistakes and pay back to others whatever is due to them.

5. Select the best of his money for the expenses of the journey.

6. Resolve to undertake his pilgrimage purely for Allahs sake.

By "the best of his money" we mean that which he knows to have been earned from perfectly legitimate sources.

A woman who intends to offer pilgrimage must be accompanied by either her husband or one of her *mahrams* or a group of reliable women.

If such a companion is available but refuses to accompany her unless she pays his expenses, she is required to pay his expenses.

If a woman takes the pilgrimage journey on her own, her pilgrimage is valid but she is not relieved of the sin of violating Islamic restrictions on the travel of a woman.

The ability to offer the pilgrimage is fulfilled if the following conditions are met:

1. Physically able.

2. Must not be too weak to travel.

3. The route must be safe. If he fears for his life or money this condition is not met.

4. He should have sufficient money to meet his necessary expenses and care for his family.

5. There should be no physical impediment which prevents him from undertaking the journey, such as imprisonment, torture or punishment inflicted by a tyrannical ruler.

There are four essentials of pilgrimage which must be done to be valid. These essentials should be ordered as follows: *ihraam* comes first, attendance at Arafat precedes the *tawaf* of *ifaadah* which, in turn, and along with shortening one's hair or shaving, are done before *sa'ie* unless one does the *sa'ie* immediately after one's first *tawaf* done on arrival at Makkah.

All pilgrims must enter into *ihraam* for the purpose of fulfilling their pilgrimage or Umrah. *Ihraam* is a state of consecration.

Ihraam starts at a certain point in time and on reaching certain locations. The point in time is between the start of Shawal until the tenth of Thul-Hajjah of the same year. This is a period of two lunar months and ten days.

If one enters into *ihraam* either before or after this period, one's pilgrimage is invalid.

As for place:
Arriving from Syria, Egypt and the west, start *ihraam*

at Al-Juhfah (Rabigh).

People of Madinah and areas beyond it start their *ihraam* at a place called Thul-Halaifah (Abyar Ali).

People from Iraq and beyond enter into *ihraam* at Thaat Irq, to the north-east of Makkah.

People of Najd, Kuwait and areas to the east and south-east have Qarn Al-Manazil (Al-Sayl).

People from Yemen and India and areas beyond begin their *ihraam* at Mount Yalamlam to the south of Mekkah.

If we connect those locations by an imaginary line, this line forms the borders of an area surrounding Makkah which is called the "hill" area.

Anyone who lands in Jeddah finds himself past the *meeqat* If one passes the *meeqat* then he must go back to the nearest *meeqat* where entry into *ihraam* is made.

If he fears he will miss the pilgrimage he proceeds with his duty and he has to atone for his mistake by slaughtering a sheep.

There are certain actions to be done before actually entering the state of *ihraam:* It is particularly recommended to have a shower or bath just before *ihraam* .

If a woman is in her menstruation period or having her postnatal discharge, then taking a bath becomes even more important.

If water is scarce, taking a bath is overlooked, a person should clean himself properly and do the other recommendations such as removing pubic and armpit hair, clipping one's nails, trimming one's moustache and keeping oneself clean.

Every man who is entering into the state of ihraam should wear special garments which are normally two pieces of clothes, preferably white, and they must not be tailored.

It is also recommended for a person entering into a state of *ihraam* to wear some perfume or something which gives a good smell.

A man may wear slippers while he is in the state of *ihraam*. If he wears shoes which cover his ankles he will need to compensate for that. He may wear shoes but it is preferable that he makes them look like slippers by binding their heels.

Doing the pilgrimage in the *tamatu* method requires each to sacrifice a sheep in gratitude to Allah. You may partake of the meat of the sacrifice.

The *tawaf* of farewell should be done as the last part of what a pilgrim does in *Mekkah.*. It must be done just before departure. When he has finished, he goes back to his place and picks up his luggage and leaves. If his departure is delayed, he repeats the *tawaf* of farewell. Omitting the *tawaf* of farewell can be compensated for by slaughtering a sheep in the Haram area.

An exception from the above ruling is given to women who happen to be in menstruation at the time when they should leave.

Once the process of pilgrimage has started, it should be completed. It is like an obligatory prayer. Once you start a prayer, you may not be interrupt it for any reason, such as opening the door or answering the telephone. You may attend to an emergency such as putting out a fire, or killing a snake or scorpion, without interrupting your prayer.

Methods of pilgrimage:
Tamattu method - if one starts with Umrah declaring as he enters into the state of consecration that he intends to do the Umrah, without mentioning pilgrimage. The term *tamattu* means "enjoyment, relaxation, comfort, convenience, etc.

Ifraad method - When one enters the state of *ihraam*, he declares his intention to do the pilgrimage and carry on with his duties "Doing one single thing."

Qiran method - To combine both duties by declaring at the time of ihraam one's intentions to do both duties together.

When the pilgrim does the Umrah first, i.e., in the *tamattu* method, completes his Umrah, he releases himself fully from *ihraam*.. All restrictions including that on sexual intercourse with his wife are lifted.

It is one of the conditions of *ihraam* for a man not to cover his head. If one covers his head for long periods during the ihraam, then he has violated its conditions and, as such, he is required to compensate by slaughtering a sheep.

Perhaps the first thing to state here is that everything which is forbidden to a Muslim in normal times is even more so during pilgrimage and particularly when the pilgrim is in the state of consecration.

It is not permissible for a person in the state of consecration to enter into a contract of marriage. He is also forbidden to have sexual intercourse with his wife or the preliminaries of sex such as kissing, etc. It is only when a person is arguing to defend Islam or Islamic position on any matter that an argument during the state of consecration is permitted.

Once a pilgrim is in *ihraam* it is no longer permissible for him to use perfume either on his garment, or his body. Nor is it permitted to wear a garment dyed with perfumery dye, such as saffron. If he takes a rose and lifts it to his nose to smell, he commits something forbidden. But if he smells some roses placed nearby, without any deliberate action of his, then this is permissible.

It is also important to emphasize that, it is not permissible to frighten an animal of game, or to point it out to someone who is not in a state of consecration, or to explain where it can be found.

If a pilgrim kills a wild animal of game in order to eat during his journey, then he has to compensate for it. The compensation in killing a pigeon is to slaughter a sheep. In the case of an ostrich, the compensation is a camel.

It is permissible for a person in the state of consecration to kill animals that could attack or injure him, such as the kite, raven, mice, scorpion or an aggressive dog. Other animals which could hurt or damage property, such as other birds of prey, wasps, bugs, fleas, flies, etc. are also permissible to kill.

Muslim women may do everything a man does including the slaughter of a sacrificial animal, as when she is on pilgrimage.

Haj and Umrah can be combined in three different ways on the same journey. The first is called *"tamattu"* which means "to enjoy something or to take advantage of it." The second is known as *qiran,* which means that both are combined together at the same time. The third method is known as *"ifraad"* and this means to have something as a single unit or action.

It should be noted here that sacrifice is a Sunnah for the *mufrid* pilgrim. That is, it is recommended but not an obligation.

It must be pointed out that since we are speaking about releasing oneself from the restrictions of the *ihraam* that there are two types of release: a limited release under which a pilgrim may wear his ordinary clothes and do all things which he is not allowed to do while in *ihraam*, with the exception of approaching his wife sexually. When this *tawaf* is done, the final release from *ihraam* is achieved and the pilgrim may have sex with his wife if they so desire.

If he performed Umrah in a time period which it normally is not performed, he will have to sacrifice a sheep in compensation.

When a man touches the body of a woman while doing the *tawaaf* in a congested crowd, his *tawaaf* and ablution remains intact. There is controversy whether touching the body of a woman nullifies the ablution. Some say not, some say it does, whilst others say it does if it is done with passion. Nothing nullifies ablution except clear proven cases.

If a man represents his mother and father to throw the *jamaraats* because of their age or sickness, he must perform his duty of stoning first and thereafter his parents. There is no rule as to whose pelting - mothers or father - should be done first.

Women perform Haj exactly as men do except for a few laws which are mentioned below:

1.) When donning the *ihraam*, a woman who is in a state of *hayd* or *nifaas*, will take a bath and don her *ihraam* at the meeqat although she is unclean;

2.) She is not permitted to enter the Masjidul Haraam or any other mosque when in this state;

3.) When she is free from her *hayad* or *nifaas*, she will remove the first ihraam she wore before entering the *meeqat*, have a bath and thereafter dress herself in a clean *ihraam*, say the *niyyah* and *talbiyyah* and thereafter   commence *tawaaf;*

4.) Women are permitted to wear sewn garments and jewelry in a state of *ihraam*,

5.) She must cover her head completely when in *ihraam*. Her face, however, must be exposed. But, if she fears *fitnah*, she should cover her face on condition that the covering does not touch her face;

6.) She will not raise her voice when saying the *talbiyyah*.. This must be done in silence;

7.) She will not hasten in the first three circumambulations of the Ka'bah as the men do, nor will she hasten her pace between the two green lights during *sa'ie*. She should walk at her normal pace;

8.) Women do not shave their heads. They will only cut as much as the first joint of the forefinger.

9.) It is obligatory for a woman who is not in a state of *hayd* or *nifaas* to perform *Tawaaful-Widaa*.

When the pilgrim draws close to the place where he has to go into *ihraam* he is recommended to have a bath or wash himself, wear some perfume, shorten his hair, remove pubic hair and the hair of his arm pits and clip nails.

It is preferable to vocalize one's intention to do the pilgrimage or the Umrah, saying: "I hereby resolve to do the pilgrimage (or the Umrah, or both of them, as the case may be) for Allah's sake. My lord make it easy for me and accept it from me."

They repeat these phrases as they go into *ihraam* and at any time they like, especially when they go up a hill or down a slope, when they meet someone, and after prayers, when they go into a car or on the back of a horse, and when they get off.

Men repeat these phrases loudly, while women lower their voices so that they are heard only by those who are close to them.

Tawaaf is to walk around the Ka'aba seven times, starting just before the black stone and going around the outside of Ka'aba. It is recommended that in the three first rounds of the *tawaaf* of arrival, men should uncover their right shoulder and run slowly as they do these rounds, if the place is not so crowded as to prevent such movement.

One round is finished every time he arrives at the black stone which a pilgrim is recommended to kiss, if he can reach it without causing any harm or inconvenience to other pilgrims.

These days, when more than thirty to forty thousand

people are engaged in *tawaaf* at the same time, any slip by any person may cause serious harm, especially if one falls down and other people trample over him without noticing him.

He is also recommended to have a drink of Zamzam water which is said by the Prophet to be "the best water on earth." "It satisfies hunger and cures illnesses."

Sa'ie is composed of walking the distance between the two hills of Safah and Marwah seven times. One starts at Safah and finishes at Marwah.

It is preferable for the one who does *sa'ie* to have ablution and to run the short distance marked with green color over the arches.

Pilgrims are recommended to go to Mina on the eighth day of Thul-Hajjah, on their way to Arafat. It is preferable if pilgrims stay that night in Mina and do not leave for Arafat until after sunrise of the ninth day of Thul-Hajjah.

The Pilgrim who performs the Haj in the *tamattu* or *giraan* methods is under obligation to slaughter an animal. This is done at Mina on the Day of Sacrifice — Yawmul-Nahi — which is the 10th Thul-Hijja.

There are the ten forbidden while the pilgrim is in the

state of Ihram:

1.) To remove or shave any body hair or part of it from the whole of the body without cause.

2.) To cut the nails either of the hands or the feet without a legitimate excuse.

3.) To cover the head.

4.) For the male pilgrim to wear even clothes as caps, socks or shirts.

5.) To make any step towards sexual intercourse as kissing, embracing, touching or even talking about sex with his wife.

6.) To make or participate in making any marriage contract.

7.) To cut, pluck or spoil the wild green plants within the Al-Haram boundary, or to hunt any edible wild animal or even to stir it up.

8.) To perform the prayers without haste and with tranquility.

9.) He must perform the Haj and Umrah rites with sincerity.

10.) All actions and sayings should be in accordance with the Quaran and Sunnah throughout his life.

Mistakes in throwing the three *Jamarat:*

1.) Some pilgrims throw the *Jamarat* with anger believing that they are devils.

2.) Some pilgrims throw the *Jamarat* with big stones or shoes or other items.

3.) Unfortunately some pilgrims make crowds and wrangle at the *Jamarat.*

4.) Throwing all the seven pebbles once will be regarded as one throw.

5.) You are not supposed to deputize somebody to

throw on your behalf unless you are weak, sick or old.

When the sun has set, pilgrims may leave Arafat to Muzdolifah. Although this departure is known as "surging on", pilgrims should take it easy as they leave.

At Muzdalifah, pilgrims pick up seven little stones to do the stoning at the grand Jamrah. They may pick up 49 stones, if they so desire, but they may equally well pick up only seven at Muzdalifah and pick up the rest at Mina.

It is recommended that as we do the stoning, that Mina should be to our right hand side and the Ka'abah to our left hand side.

After stoning the Jamrah, it is time for pilgrims to slaughter the animals they want to sacrifice. Each pilgrim, man or woman, who has taken advantage of offering the Umrah either before the pilgrimage or together with it, is required to sacrifice a lamb or a goat or, alternatively, seven pilgrims may share in the sacrifice of one camel or a cow.

After the sacrifice, the pilgrims may shave their heads or shorten their hair. To shave one's head is much better, because the Prophet prayed for those who shaved three times before he included those who shortened their hair.

At Mina, as they do the stoning, they start with the little *Jamrah*, the nearest to Mina, then the middle one, and finish with the grand one. This stoning is symbolic of the pilgrim's determination not to yield to the temptations of Satan when he tries to lure him away from the path of piety. A pilgrim must try to hit the place with each stone.

If a pilgrim omits the duty of attendance at Arafat, that is, if he does not arrive at Arafat before the break of dawn on the Day of Sacrifice, his pilgrimage is invalid. He must complete the duties of Umrah namely, *tawaf* and *sa' ie* and himself from ihraam by shaving his head or shortening his hair. He must do the pilgrimage the following year and atone for the omission by slaughtering a sheep or a goat.

If a pilgrim omits *sa'ie,* he may do it as long as he is in Makkah or close to it. If he has gone back home, and he lives a long distance away from Makkah, he does not return to do the sa'ie. He arranges, instead for a sheep or a goat to be sacrificed in the "Haram" area on his behalf.

If a pilgrim has sexual intercourse with his wife before the first, limited release from ihraam, his pilgrimage is invalid. He must, however, complete the duties of pilgrimage and slaughter a cow or a camel, and he must also repeat his pilgrimage the following year.

He who is physically prevented from completing his pilgrimage, or Umrah, or both, having gone into *ihraam*, should slaughter a sheep at the place where his prevention occurs and release himself from *ihraam*. If no sheep is available he can substitute for it food bought for the same price as a sheep. If he cannot afford that, he fasts one day for each "mudd" (an Arabian measure).

It is not necessary when the *tawaf* of farewell is finished to walk backward, with one's face toward the Kaaba as some people do. This was not reported to have been done by the Prophet or his companions. Hence, it is an innovation and no innovations are admitted into Islamic worship.

There is no specified limit or duration for visiting Madinah. A short visit is as good as a long visit except for these two facts:

1. In a longer stay in Madinah, one may greet the Prophet several times.

2. Each prayer in the Prophet's Mosque is rewarded as highly as one thousand prayers anywhere else, with the exception of the Sacred Mosque in Makkah.

If a duty of pilgrimage is missed, it is compensated for by sacrificing a sheep. If a recommended practice is overlooked or missed, it needs no compensation. Thus, if you do the stoning wrongly or you miss it, you have to compensate for it by sacrificing a sheep. If you do not spend the night in Mina you either sacrifice a sheep if you follow one of the schools of thought which considers it a duty, or you do not have to sacrifice it if you take the other view.

We have to differentiate between a duty of pilgrimage and one of its essentials. An essential obligation is one that must be done by all pilgrims. If it is missed, it cannot be compensated for in any way, unless there is time to go back and do it. The essentials are three according to most scholars. (1) The intention to complete the pilgrimage at the point of meeqat. (2) Attendance at Arafat on the 9th of Thul-Hajjah. (3) The *tawaf* of *ifaadah*. Some scholars also consider the sa'ie between the hills of As-Safa and Al-Mawah an essential, while others consider it a duty.

Certain prayers are offered on pilgrimage days differently from the way they are offered in normal days. This is due to the fact that the Prophet offered them in that way when he offered his pilgrimage.

Islam requires that a woman should not travel a distance which is normally covered in a whole day without being accompanied by her husband or a relative whom she may not marry. Several prominent scholars have pointed out that if a woman cannot find a *mahram* to travel with she may undertake the journey to do the pilgrimage if she is traveling with "trustworthy company." Traveling by plane is considered to satisfy the requirement of "trustworthy company" since the airlines are duty bound to take good care of their passengers.

The two issues of visa regulations and validity of pilgrimage are separate. When Allah considers the validity of our pilgrimage, He does not question us on compliance with administrative rules. He accepts our efforts when we make them for His sake. The fact that his keenness leads him to commit a legal offensive in order to fulfill ambition does not reduce his reward for pilgrimage.

The Talbiya: "Here I am, Oh Lord, here I am, here I am. There is no partner unto Thee, here I am. No doubt all praise and goodness is for Thee and the Sovereignty. There is no partner unto Thee."

It is not true that you cannot release yourself from the state of consecration until you have offered the sacrifice. Indeed, the sacrifice has nothing to do with this release. The release is made on the 10th of Thul-Hajjah, after you have done any two of the three duties which are required of you on that day, namely, the stoning at the Grand Jamrah, the tawaf of ifaadah and the shaving of your head or shortening of your hair.

With the Haj barely a few days away, the Ministry of Interior has warned that carrying of books, pictures and pamphlets of political propaganda or ideological content is absolutely forbidden and that "anyone who is found possessing any of these ... will be punished and subject to regulations in force in the kingdom, with no leniency or forbearance." The statement appears in the latest publication, entitled *Pilgrimage Organizing Instructions*.

The Standing at Arafat, representing the climax of the Haj, will be on Friday, June 21, 1991. The announcement carried in the press, said Thursday, June 13, 1991, is the first day of the Islamic month of Dhul Hijjah as the moon was sighted last night by two peoples.

It is strange that many people tend to think that one has to keep the same garments of *ihraam* throughout the period of pilgrimage, even though they may get very dirty. There is indeed no good reason for that. It is perfectly permissible for anyone to change the *ihraam* garments for no purpose other than cleanliness. It goes without saying that if an impurity falls on ihraam garments, it must be washed off and the garment itself must be properly washed. A spare set will be very handy.

A *fidyah* is the flow of blood of a sheep or goat in which the rules of the Quirbaan are applied. This is known as a *Dumm.* or the feeding of six poor, or needy people, or fasting for three days. The above of course has rules attached to it:

1) Perfume If anyone uses this while in the *A'maal* (actions) of Haj, he should give a *fidyah* by slaughtering a sheep. 2) Wearing any type of stitched clothing or underpants or shoes or even a turban or any type of stitched clothing that goes around the body. If any of these are done, a *fidyah* is then obligatory. This clause has two rules attached to it: (a) That the person should know it is Haraam. If he does not know it is Haraam, no *fidyah* is then *waajib.* (b) That these acts are committed before the first Tahleel. If it is done afterwards, no *fidyah* is *waajib.* 3) When the person cuts the hair or the nails. 4) Kissing and fondling. If this is done before the Tahleels, then a *fidyah* is *waajib.* This must be done in such a way that it nullifies the wudhu. 5) To apply oil to the hair or beard. If the oil is applied unknowingly, no fidyah is required. Moreover,

the person should know it is haraam. If he was unaware
thereof, again, no *fidyah* would be required.

At Muzdalifah the *maghrib* and *eshaa salaah* will be
performed during the time of *eshaa*, with one *adhaan* and one
iqamah. The *niyyah* for the *maghrib salaah* will be made as
adaa and not *gadhaa*. The time for these two *salaah* com-
mences approximately one and one half hours after sunset. No
sunnah or *nafl* must be performed between the *fardh* of *maghrib*
and *eshaa*. Immediately after the three *rak'ah fardh of maghrib*
perform the *fardh of eshaa*.

When you arrive at Makkah, go directly to the Sacred
Mosque and do your *tawaf* of arrival, walking round the Kaabah
seven times.

8th Thul-Hajjah

You are recommended to go to Mina and stay the night
there before you proceed to Arafat.

9th Thul-Hajjah

Try as much as much as you can to be present at Arafat
before sunset. Pray Dhuhr and Asr together, in their shortened
form after sunset, proceed from Arafat to Muzdalifah and pray
Maghrib and Isha as a delayed combination. Stay the night at
Muzdalifah until shortly before sunrise.

10th Thul-Hajjah

You should proceed to Mina and do your first stoning at
the Jamrah of Aqabah at any time between dawn and midday.
If the method is tamattu' or qiran, slaughter a sheep. Shave
your head, or shorten your hair. Go to Makkah to do your tawaf
of ifaadah. Restrictions are lifted.

11th Thul-Hajjah

You have to do the stoning at the three Jamrahs, starting with the little one. You have to spend the night at Mina.

12th Thul-Hajjah

You do the stoning at the three Jamrahs in the same way as you done on the 11th of Thul-Hajjah. When you have finished your stoning, you may leave Mina, provided you are out of the boundary of Mina before sunset. When you arrive at Makkah, you do the tawaf of ifaadah. Again, you have to do the sa'ie if you have not done it after the tawaf of arrival or the tawaf of ifaadah. Otherwise, all your duties of pilgrimage are completed.

Three days at Arafat, Makkah and Mina are sufficient to fulfill the duties of pilgrimage.

More than 200,000 Australian sheep imported live for sacrifice in Algeria have provoked a row on whether their lack of tails bars them from religious sacrifice. Imported at a total cost of $15 Million, they are being sold for $165 a head compared with around $385 for the local beasts. Algerian newspapers today reported suggestions that regional sheep "barons" had started rumors that the sheep — castrated and without tails — were not religiously acceptable for sacrifice during Eid. Local fatwa — religious rulings — have banned their sacrifice in some areas. A spokesman for the regional meat board told the newspapers: "We only concluded the purchase after agreement with the Supreme Islamic Council of Australia which judged the beasts conformed to standards demanded for the sacrifice." But Algeria's Supreme Islamic Council said: "Sheep whose tails have been cut completely, or more than one-third, are not authorized for sacrifice." The sheep could, however, be eaten.

A group of Jeddah residents decided to perform Haj this year to have the great reward of making pilgrimage on a Friday, which was destined to occur this year. But they did not want to spend much on the trip, and planned to stay most of the day in Jeddah and return to the holy place of Mina in the night. However, one night they slept fast and sound, thus forgot or failed to return to Mina that night, which cost each of them the price of a sheep to make up the lapsed night. They slaughtered eight sheep in Jeddah and ate the meat, leaving some of it as charity to the poor. It was unacceptable to do that, and when they were told that they should slay sheep in Makkah and must not eat any of it, they paid the price and slaughtered sheep once again. They saved zero.

It is a condition when slaughtering a Hadee, to make sure that the Hadee is free from the following:

a) That it should be free from sickness.

b) That it should not be too skinny.

c) That it should not be blind.

d) That it should not be one eyed.

e) That it should not be so sick that it has no marrow in its bones.

f) That it should not be lame or cripple.

More than 500,000 sheep and 25,000 cattle and camels were to be slaughtered Saturday at the start of the Eid al-

Adha (feast of the sacrifice) that marks the end of the pilgrimage.

Q. During my pilgrimage I did the tawaf of ifaadah on the 11th of Thul-Hajjah, and completed the tawaf of farewell on the following day. After the tawaf of farewell I saw a semblance of semen on my clothes, but I did not remember having any wet dream. What should I do?

A. Since you have seen what clearly indicates that you must have had an ejaculation, and you do not remember having had a wet dream on that day or on previous days, you have to act on what is certain. That means, in this case, that you have been for some time in the state of ceremonial impurity. You should count that from the last time you slept before discovering the semen in your clothes. Thus, if you had slept between performing the two tawafs, then the first one is correct and the second one was done when you were in the state of ceremonial impurity. On the other hand, if you went to sleep after you had completed the tawaf of farewell, then that tawaf is correct and valid, while your prayers after the last sleep you had remain valid. You have to repeat all obligatory prayers and other types of worship for which ablution is needed, such as tawaf, which you performed between walking up after your last sleep and the time when you had a grand ablution, or ghusl. If that included the tawaf of farewell, then that tawaf needs to be repeated. Since the time of pilgrimage is over, then you have to compensate for it by slaughtering a sheep in the Haram area and distributing its meat to the poor there. You may not partake of its meat. You should also repeat your prayers which you may have performed during that period.

RAMADAN

All good actions are rewarded more generously when they are done during the month of Ramadan.

Your fast is not affected if you start the day in a state of ceremonial impurity, or if you go to sleep during the day and you have a wet dream. You should proceed to remove that state of ceremonial impurity by taking a bath.

The importance is that every good action is rewarded by Allah ten times its value. When we fast the month of Ramadan, we are rewarded for fasting ten months. If we fast six more days, we have the reward of fasting sixty days.

A woman who does not fast during her menstruation period in Ramadan should compensate for those days of nonfasting first.

A traveler who arrives home is allowed to eat and drink after his arrival as travelers are not required to fast.

If his wife is not fasting for a legitimate reason, then both of them are not fasting. As such, if they have intercourse, they commit no offense.

During the Ramadan day a Muslim is not allowed to eat, drink or have sex in normal circumstances.

Fasting in Ramadan is compulsory upon every Muslim, male or female, who has these qualifications: 1. To be mentally and physically fit, which means to be sane and able; 2. To be of full age, the age of puberty and discretion, which is normally about fourteen; 3. To be present at your permanent settlement, your home town, your farm, your business premises, etc. This means not to be traveling on a journey of about fifty miles or more; 4. To be fairly certain that the fasting is unlikely to cause you any harm, physical or mental, other than the normal reactions to hunger, thirst, etc.

One of seven exceptions includes women in the period of menstruation or in confinement. These are not allowed to fast even if they can and want to.

The fast of any day of Ramadan becomes void by intentionally eating, drinking or smoking or indulgence in intimate marital intercourse. If done deliberately the penalty is to observe the fast of sixty consecutive days or feed sixty poor persons sufficiently.

If anyone, by mistake, does something that would ordinarily break fast, his observance is not nullified, and his fast stands valid provided he stops doing that thing the moment he realizes what he is doing.

If one eats, drinks, or has intercourse, thinking that the sun has set or that *fajr* has not occurred that person is to make up that day.

The only action, according to most scholars, which requires that both the day be made up and the act of expiation be performed is having sexual intercourse during the day of Ramadan.

Most scholars say that both men and women have to perform the acts of expiation if they intentionally have intercourse during a day of Ramadan on which they had intended to fast.

If the woman was forced to have intercourse by the man, the expiation will be obligatory only upon the man.

If they had intercourse out of forgetfulness or not due to choice then the expiation is not obligatory on either of them.

If one has intercourse twice during a day, before performing the expiation for the first act, then he need only perform one act of expiation. If he has performed the expiation for the first one, then he need not perform an act of expiation for the second, according to most scholars.

If one dies and has some fasts to make up, then his guardian should fast on his behalf.

If the new moon is sighted in a country and people there started fasting, but if it was not sighted in another country, then there are several cases to be considered:

Case one: If two countries are united under a single ruler or government and the time of c iafbo the same in both countries, then when the new moon is sighted in one of the countries and confirmed by their common ruler, all people in the two countries, without exception, must start their fasting.

Case two: If two countries are far in distance from each other, have different times of rising of celestial bodies and are not under the same ruler or government, then people in one of them are not obligated to fast on the sighting of the moon in the other.

Case three: If a country in which the moon was not sighted is far in distance, and has different times of rising of celestial bodies from a country in which the moon was sighted, then people in the former country are not obliged to start fasting even if the ruler of the two countries is the same.

Case four: If the two countries are close to one another in distance and have the same time of rising of celestial bodies, but are under different rulers, then people in one of them are not in general obligated to start the fast on the sighting of the moon in the other.

Those who believe the sighting testimony reported by the neighboring country may start fasting, but those who do not believe it do not have to start fasting.

So, worship times differ according to the difference in the time of the rising of celestial bodies. The more countries are far apart in distance, the more different will be their times of worship such as prayer, fasting, etc. This is due to the geographical locations on the globe along different longitudes and latitudes.

Some scholars say that the five prescribed prayer times occur at every hour on earth, because there is sunset or sunrise at every hour at some point on earth owing to the fact that the earth is round and rotates around the sun.

Making amends for the offences are called kaffarah (atonement, redemption, repentance, expiration, compensatory act). Islam introduced a new animal sacrifice. It is a complete break away from the pagan practice of 'appeasing' deities by slaughtering animals in their names or by mere chanting of prayer. "It is not their meat, nor their blood that reaches Allah, it is your piety that reaches Him."

Kaffarah becomes due if we willfully violate the Ramadan Fast through any one of the following acts:
1. If we eat, drink, smoke or in any way break this fast willfully.
2. If we have sexual relation with our wife while observing the fast of Ramadan.

Using a suppository during the day of fasting does not invalidate your fast. What is forbidden us during the day of fasting is eating, drinking and sex. Using a suppository does not come under any of these three headings. The same applies to using eye, ear or nasal drops or using an inhaler for asthma or a nasal spray. None of these invalidates fasting.

SCIENCE

Foremost amongst the scientists in the study of embryology are Islamic physicians. An Islamic book *Human Development As Revealed In The Quran and Hadith* is indeed a testimony verifying the authenticity of the Quran. Whereas nobody had knowledge of this subject until fairly recently, the Quran gives a graphic description of every stage of the development of the fetus.

Isn't it incredible that the sense of hearing, seeing, and feeling develop in that particular order as described in the Quran. The primordial of the internal ears appear before the beginning of the eyes and the brain differentiates last.

We understand that "Allah has made every living thing out of water." This is a very important truism which tells us that water is the origin of all life. The Qur'an was revealed 14 centuries ago, when no human being even remotely linked the origin of life with water. Today, we accept this as fact easily because we know that water is the predominant element in all living creatures. Moreover, it is the environment in which life originated. Scientists did not discover that until recently.

The truthfulness of the Qur'an is not subject to proof by science and scientists. If we hear today of a scientific discovery which confirms what is mentioned in the Qur'an, we are not overjoyed. Everything mentioned in the Qur'an is true, although it may contradict the finding of human knowledge.

References to stars, planets and skies in the Qur'an have preceded contemporary science in stressing that the universe is too vast for our minds to imagine.

No one can deny the fact that the scientific verses of all the Holy books are the foundation of science education, which stress the spirit of enquiry and study of nature, while the Quran gives us more clear expounding being the last Holy Book. Any confusion should not occur regarding the detailing of scientific references as the references in the Quran are truly verbatim. There are six more planets in space on which life exists as on our earth planet. The seven number of living earth (planets) are existing in the universe including ours, and they are arranged very systematically and scientifically in the circular arrangement tied together with the rope of magnetic attraction. There is an earth (planet) in the deep North of our planet and one in the deep South. Each living earth planet is placed at an equal distance of approximately 10,368,000,000 km from each other, which I calculated by deriving the formula as below:

$D = 40\ P\ X\ S$

$= 40 \times 500 \times 12 \times 30 \times 24 \times S$

$= 20,000 \times 360 \times 24 \times S$

$= 172,800,000 \times 60$

= 10,368,000,000 km

D = Distance between two earths

40 = Constant of formula

P = Period of travel (500 year)

S = Speed of Horse (60km)

For many years scientists and researchers have been scanning the universe to find other living planets, but till now no success has been achieved. If the above guideline is followed, the day will not be far off when it will be acknowledged by all that there is life on seven planets.

There are other modern scientific reasons given for prayer system of Islam. Some of them are that regular physical exercise is considered good for maintaining health. Five-time daily prayers fulfill that requirement. First, salat requires full concentration. Hands folded on chest or abdomen help in concentrating mind and attention to one point. In ruku' — bending while still standing - muscles or abdomen and back experience contraction and legs and feet are expanded. In sujoud - bending the body in sitting position while putting the forehead on the ground — is another posture for expanding the muscles of the back, contracting muscles of abdomen, and both contracting and expanding the muscles of neck, legs, feet, while balancing the upper limbs. In the tashahhud position — sitting on folded legs and lower toes , the upper body relaxes while the legs are stretched and carry the load of the full body, firming up muscles. More can be said about this aspect of Islamic prayers.

The Quran brought humanity from pre-scientific age to the age of rationalism. The Prophet was born in the midst of idolatry and polytheism of Mekkah. He was very much perturbed over the idol worship of his folk. He used to go to the Hira Cave for meditation. It was there at the age of 40 that he received the first revelation "Read in the name of the Lord Who created, Who created man from something that clings, Read!" The very first line invites our attention to the Creator and His creation. Disclosing a scientific fact, the Quran said, the man is created with something that clings. There are other verses to which explain the processing of the embryo. "Verily We created man from a drop of mingled liquids to test him ..." "He began the creation of man from clay. Then He made his progeny from a quintessence of despised liquid." "Was he not a drop of fluid (sperm out of semen) which gushed forth?" Thereafter he became Alaqa (something that clings)..." Aristotle (384-322 BC) thought that creation and formation of the embryo was from the menstrual blood. To him the process resembled the curdling of milk into cheese. In the first quarter of the 7th century CE the Quran brushed off the views of Aristotle telling that Allah created man from a drop of mingled liquids - amshaj - of both male and female. However, Europe remained stuck to the notions of Aristotle, until Redi in 1668 dealt a blow to his theory and Pasteur in 1864 wrote the final obituary to the doctrine. Later Van Banden in 1883 proved that both male and female participated equally in the formation of the human zygote. Thus what was said in the Quran, was finally upheld by the scientists after about 1,300 years of scientific ignorance regarding the creation of man. It is also proved that the total semen ejaculated contains an average of 200 to 300 million of spermatozoa, only one out of them fertilizes the ovum to form the zygote which grows into a baby. The Arabic word nutfa translates as a drop of liquid is singular, thus nutfa is that spermatozoa which causes fertilization. The words nutfatain amsbaj further establishes that male spermatozoa mixed with female cell causes fertilization to form the zygote. This fertilization stage is described in the word alag, something that attaches to the uterus. The Quran describes the next stage as mudgha meaning the chewed lump - a mass having teeth mark on it. In the early 7th century, no one knew the stages of embryo's development. Only in the 20th century the scientists could observe it. One has, therefore, to accept that the Quran is the book of God.

An international symposium on the best means of tackling cracks appearing in buildings in the Arab World will be organized by the ministry of Public Works. Participants in the symposium which aims at exchanging information and experience in this matter at the regional and international levels will debate the causes of the phenomena and propose solutions to the problem.

A Saudi technician recently designed a low-cost, innovative air cooler now being studied by a local firm for possible commercial production. He calls his air cooler invention "Al Hajj" which releases air cooled by two liters of potable water. Working five hours a day from May to July this year, he assembled scrap materials, an electric fan, plastic and a few electric parts to come up with the 3 kg, square portable unit that can effectively cool an average sized living room. Inside a square, transparent plastic box a turning fan blows out air cooled by water circulating through small pipes, and finally draining to a compressed mat of wood shavings.

The Directorate General of Traffic is conducting a study aimed at replacing the existing vehicular plate registration system by reducing the plate digits from seven to four. The study is being carried out in conjunction with the National Safety Board. The introduction of the new system is dictated by organizational considerations and is meant to facilitate easy reading and registration of the plates.

It is permissible for a Muslim to have a blood transfusion using the blood of a non-Muslim who smokes, eats pork and drinks alcohol. The fact that the blood donor is a non-Muslim does not affect the permissibility of giving that blood to a Muslim. The pork he had eaten and the intoxicants he had drunk do not make his blood contaminated in a way to prevent its use by a Muslim.

PERSONAL OBSERVATIONS

Prayers are called five times a day. *Fajr* (Dawn) can be as early as 3:50 a.m., *Dhuhr* (Noon) around twelve thirty, *Asr* (Afternoon) about three thirty, *Maghrib* (Sunset) at sunset and *Isha* (Night) usually about one and one half hour after sunset.

All commerce stops four times a day at prayer call for twenty to thirty minutes. Shops close, customers are asked to leave some restaurants, nothing is sold, traded or bought during prayer call. All trips to town to take care of business must be planned around prayer call. Most places close at *Dhuhr* and do not open until after *Asr*. The *Matawas* patrol the streets looking for offenders not attending prayer call.

During Operation Desert Shield and Storm the *matawas* were somewhat muted in their enthusiasm to harass women not in *habias*. In one case a *matawas* switched the bare legs of a female Marine only to be decked by her. In another case a female Security Policeman walked through the unit Mosque on her way to the cafeteria for lunch. She was refused service. After waiting patiently she finally rested her M-16 on the tray line, cleared the breach and said she wanted a cheese burger and fries and wanted them now. Some say her actions were unintentional but she did get served.

If enthusiasm for enforcing Islamic traditions was muted during Desert Storm, they more than made up for it following the withdrawal of Western troops.

GLOSSARY OF TERMS

'habl Allah - the rope of Allah.

alakah - something that clings

anthan - call to prayer.

apostacy -(apostasy), An abandonment of
one's religious faith.

Al-Qasswaa' - Mohammad's she camel.

Aqeedah - belief.

aqeeqah - sacrifice offered in gratitude for
the birth of a child.

Asr - afternoon prayer.

Athan - one call for prayer.

Awqaf - endowments.

Awrah - the part of the body, man and woman,
that must not be seen by others.

baatiel - null and void.

bida - interest.

bismillah - in the name of Allah.

dar al-harb - land war.

Dhu Al Qa'dah - eleventh month of the Islamic
calendar.

Dhu Al Hijiah - twelfth month of the Islamic
calendar. the month in which the
Haj holiday period occurs.

Dhuhr - noon prayer

dower - an amount of money, in cash or kind

which is payable to the wife by the husband
at the time the marriage contract is made.

fatwa - religious ruling.

Fajr - dawn prayer.

Figh - jurisprudence; the Islamic system of law.

ghusl - grand ablution.

ghutra - head covering.

halaal - permissible.

haraam - forbidden.

Hejab - full veiling.

hijab - the veil.

Ibadat - Submission to Allah as your Master and
you are His slave.

igamah - shortened form of the anthan. call to prayer.

Isha - night prayer.

Istigfar - forgiveness.

I'tihaf - confinement, delay, to stay behind or to
practice selfrestraint.

iqamat - second call for prayer.

Jahiliyyah - the period of ignorance.

Jamada I - fifth month of the Islamic calendar.

Jamada II - sixth month of the Islamic calendar.

jiwar - neighbor or neighborhood.

kafer - non-believer.

khulaa - the breakfast of the marriage at the
wife's request.

khula - nullification of a marriage.

Khutba - exposition on the philosophy and
significance of Haj.

Kuf' - someone of equivalent social status.

kufr - disbelief.

Maghrib - sunset prayer.

Mahram - those of her relatives whom she cannot
marry.

meeqat - starting point for pilgrimage.

modgha - chewed lump.

Mu'allim - a guide who instructs the pilgrim where, when and how to observe things.

mudad - an Arabian measure. Spelled as mudd in the text.

mudd - see mudad.

Muharram - first month of the Islamic calendar.

mufrid - a pilgrim who opts for the "ifraad" method of combining the Haj and Umrah.

muta - a marriage with a "time term" in the agreement.

nutfah - a drop of fluid (sperm).

pardah - the name of a special dress that Muslim women wear.

pbuh - peace be upon him.

Rabi I - third month of the Islamic calendar.

Rabi II - fourth month of the Islamic calendar.

Rajab - seventh month of the Islamic calendar.

Ramadan - ninth month of the Islamic calendar. The month in which fasting is done.

sadaqah - charitable donation.

Safar - second month of the Islamic calendar.

Salaah - prayer.

Sha'ban - eighth month of the Islamic calendar.

Shari'ah - the injunctions of Islam as laid down in the Holy Qur'an and Sunnah.

Shawwal - tenth month of the Islamic calendar.

shoat - circuit.

sunnah - method, way, practice. The practice chosen by the prophet and recommended by him.

tafsir - Interpretation of the Quran.

talbiyah - phrases declaring that they are responding to Allah's call and that they declare their belief in Allah's unity.

taqwah - God-consciousness with the rope of Allah.
Taraiq - the way or the orbit of a planet.
taubah - forgiveness.
Tauheed - the Oneness of God Almighty.
tawaf - the encompassing of the sacred Home.
ummah - the Muslim majority countries.
waaf - property belonging to Allah and not to man.
waleemah - a dinner given shortly after marriage
                (also wallema).
wallema - a dinner which the bridegroom gives
                within a few days of his wedding.
zakaah - a compulsory pay-out to the needy.
ziyarah - visit

ʃ